NEW & SELECTED POEMS

1974–1994

NEW & SELECTED POEMS

1974–1994

Stephen Dunn

W.W. NORTON & COMPANY

NEW YORK / LONDON

The text of this book is composed in 11/ 13 Bembo
with the display set in Centaur
Composition and Manufacturing by the Maple- Vail Book Manufacturing Group.
Book design by Jam Design

Library of Congress Cataloging- in- Publication Data
Dunn, Stephen, 1939–
    [Poems. Selections]
    New & selected poems : (1974–1994) / Stephen Dunn.
        p.   cm.
    Includes index.
    I. Title.   II. Title: New and selected poems.
PS3554. U49N49   1994
811 ´. 54—dc20   93- 33212

ISBN 0- 393- 31300- X
ISBN 978-0-393-31300-0
W. W. Norton & Company, Inc., 500 Fifth Avenue, New York, N.Y. 10110
www.wwnorton.com

W. W. Norton & Company Ltd., Castle House, 75/76 Wells Street, London W1T 3QT

20 19 18 17 16 15 14 13 12 11

For Lois, Andrea, and Susanne

Contents

From *Work and Love* (1981)

From *Not Dancing* (1984)

Acknowledgments

Poems in this volume have appeared in the
  following books:

Looking for Holes in the Ceiling, University of
  Massachusetts Press, 1974.
Full of Lust and Good Usage (1976), *A Circus of
  Needs* (1978), *Work and Love* (1981), and *Not
  Dancing* (1984) were published by Carnegie-
  Mellon University Press.
Local Time, William Morrow, 1986.
Between Angels (1989) and *Landscape at the
  End of the Century* (1991) were published by
  W. W. Norton.

The new poems have appeared or will appear in the
  following journals:

The American Poetry Review: "Some Things I
  Wanted to Say to You."
Antaeus: "Something Like Happiness."
The Georgia Review: "The Observer,"
  "The Woman with Five Hearts," and "Afterlife."
The Graham House Review: "Honesty" and
  "Night Truths."
The Kenyon Review: "Decorum."
The Nation: "Wind in a Jar."
The Paris Review: "A Good Life" and "The
  Vanishings."
Poetry: "Beautiful Women" and "The Snowmass
  Cycle."
The Southern Review: "The Resurrection" and
  "A Petty Thing."

"The Vanishings" was selected for *Best American
  Poetry 1993.*

"The best way to know life
is to love many things."

—*Vincent Van Gogh*

"The greater the love, the
more false to its object . . ."

—*W. H. Auden*

Homage to the Divers

from A CIRCUS OF NEEDS

A love poem at the bottom
of the sea, in a treasure ship,
reachable, yes,
we must believe reachable.
In an air-tight container
somewhere in the captain's quarters,
somewhere off Hatteras,
written by . . .
And a key in a skeleton's hand
and the whole world up above
diving for it,
some with all the equipment,
some holding their breath.

New Poems

The Snowmass Cycle

for Laure-Anne Bosselaar and Kurt Brown

1. RETREAT

The sailor dreamt of loss,
but it was I who dreamt the sailor.
I was landlocked, sea-poor.
The sailor dreamt of a woman
who stared at the sea, then tired
of it, advertised her freedom.
She said to her friend: I want
all the fire one can have
without being consumed by it.
Clearly, I dreamt the woman too.
I was surrounded by mountains
suddenly green after a long winter,
a chosen uprootedness, soul shake-up,
every day a lesson about the vastness
between ecstasy and repose.
I drank coffee called Black Forest
at the local cafe. I took long walks
and tried to love the earth
and hate its desecrations.
All the Golden Retrievers wore red
bandannas on those muttless streets.
All the birches, I think, were aspens.
I do not often remember my dreams,
or dream of dreamers in them.
To be without some of the things
you want, a wise man said,
is an indispensable part of happiness.

2. MOUNTAIN, SKY

I've been paying attention
to the sky again.
I've seen a ravine up there,
and a narrow, black gorge.

Not to worry, I tell myself,
about tricks the mind plays,
as long as you know they're tricks.

If the rich are casually cruel
perhaps it's because
they can stare at the sky
and never see an indictment
in the shape of clouds.

The frown, for example,
in a thunderhead. The fist.

That big mountain
I've been looking at—
I love how it borrows purple
from the filtered light,
sometimes red.

Like any of us
it's all of its appearances.

It's good that the rich
have to die,
a peasant saying goes,
otherwise they'd live forever.

Here in this rented house,
high up, I understand.
I'm one of the rich
for a while. The earth feels
mine and the air I breathe
is rarefied, if thin.

Dusk now is making its last claim.
I love the confluence

of dark mountain, dark sky.
Soon I won't know the beginning
from the end.

3. HIM

Those empty celebrations of the half-believer
along for the ride.
Those secret words repeated in mirrors—
someone's personal fog.
A man's heart ransomed for comfort
or a few extra bucks, his soul in rags.

I have been him and him and him.

Was it nobility or senility
when my old grandmother tried to drown
artificial flowers in the bathtub?

Can only saints carry the load
without talking about the burden?

I want to lean into life,
catch the faintest perfume.

In every boy child an old man is dying.
By middle age
he begins to stink, complain.

I want to have gifts for him
when we finally meet.
I want him to go out like an ancient
Egyptian, surrounded
by what is his, desiring nothing.

4. DELINEATION AT DUSK

A lost hour, and that animal lassitude
after a vanished afternoon.
Outside: joggers, cyclists.
Motion, the great purifier, is theirs.
If this were Europe someone in a tower
might be ringing a bell.
People hearing it would know
similar truths, might even know
exactly who they are.
It's getting near drinking time.
It's getting near getting near;
a person alone conjures rules
or can liquefy, fall apart.
That woman with the bouffant—
chewing gum, waiting for the bus—
someone thinks she's beautiful.
It's beautiful someone does.
The sky's murmuring, the storm
that calls you up,
makes promises, never comes.
Somewhere else, no doubt,
a happy man slicing a tomato,
a woman with a measuring cup.
Somewhere else: the foreclosure
of a feeling or a promise,
followed by silence or shouts.
Here, the slow dance of contingency,
an afternoon connected to an evening
by a slender wish. Sometimes absence
makes the heart grow sluggish
and desire only one person, or one thing.
I am closing the curtains.
I am helping the night.

5. SOLITUDE

A few days ago I stopped looking
at the photographs
clustered on the wall, nudes,
which had become dull to me,
like a tourist's collection of smooth rocks.

I turned away from the view
and conjured a plague of starlings.
Oh how they darkened the landscape.

Surely such beauty had been waiting for its elegy.
I felt like crushing a rhododendron.

Now and again I feel the astonishment
of being alive like this, in this body,
the ventricles and the small bones
in the hand, the intricacies of digestion. . . .

When the radio said parents in California
gave birth to another child
so that their older child might have
a bone-marrow transplant and *live,*

I found myself weeping
for such complicated beauty.
How wonderful the radio
and its distant, human voices.

The rain now is quite without consequence
coming down.

I suppose I've come to the limits
of my paltry resources, this hankering

for people and for massive disturbance,
then high pressure,
the sequence that's been promised for days.

I will long to be alone
when my friends arrive.

6. THE BODY WIDENS

The body widens, and people are welcomed
into it, many at a time. This must be
what happens when we learn to be generous
when we're not in love, or otherwise charmed.
I've been examining yesterday's ashes. I've visited
my own candleless altar. Little by little,
the old selfish parts of me are loosening.
I have a plan for becoming lean: to use
all my fat in service of expansion. Have women
always known this? Loveliness and fear
when they open and let in and give away?
The mountains here pierce the sky,
and the sky, bountiful, closes in around them.

7. A NEW MOUTH

Give me a new mouth; I want to talk.
I've been watching the spider mend its web.
I think I've learned something
about architecture from a swallow.
Excuse me while I separate the nettles
from the flowers, while I put my nose
to the black moist smell of earth
and come up smiling. Somewhere in the world
is the secret name

for God, many-lettered, unpronounceable.
        There's a speakable grace
in the fields and even in the cities.
The grapes ripen, someone refuses to become
a machine. And yet I want to talk
about the worn-out husks of men and women
returning from the factories,
the venereal streets, the bruise history
passes down to its forlorn children.
        I need a new mouth to acknowledge
that piety will keep us small, imprisoned,
that it's all right to be ridiculous
and sway first to the left, then to the right,
in order to find our balance.
                        I've been watching
an evening star quiver. I've been trying
to identify the word before its utterance.
Give me a new mouth and I'll be
a guardian against forgetfulness.
I've noticed the wind doesn't discriminate
between sycamore and cypress.
I want to find the cool, precise language
for how passion gives rise to passion.

8. STRANGER

The wind gone. I can hear my breathing.
I can hear the lateness of the hour
by what isn't moving.

Woodrun Slope. Snowmass Village.
These are winter names, and it's summer.
The water from the mountains
rushes down man-made gullies.

Serious phantoms with their black tears
are out tonight.
I'm close—my other delusion goes—
to the heart of things.

A young man with a young man's itch
would rise and go out prowling.

Tomorrow I'll choose a mountain
that's a hill, take the slowest horse
at the Lazy-7, slow and old,
sure to know its trail.

I knew a man who said he could dominate
solitude. In other ways, too,
he was a fool.

Once I wanted to be
one of those fabulous strangers
who appear and disappear.
Now I arrive only by invitation,
stay long enough to earn my fare.

Outside my window, clouds from the west
erasing the stars.
A coyote howling its singular news.

At whatever pace,
isn't there an imperative to live?

Before a person dies he should experience
the double fire
of what he wants and shouldn't have.

The Observer

There ought to be behind the door of every happy, contented man
someone standing with a hammer, continually reminding him with
a tap that there are unhappy people.

—*Anton Chekhov*

Beyond my terrace and its five stone steps
    was the beginning of the world.

I would delay entry into it once again,
    watch the crows

noisy in the white pines, look for deer
    in the distant field.

Pornography, I thought, must have begun like this,
    a man with lots of time

trying out one thing, then another, until
    what interested him

was only a dull thrill of watching. I had good
    binoculars and a naked eye.

On certain blue days, I'd bring the blue closer
    where it would whiten, cease to exist.

One day, inside, watching the Olympics, I'd wept
    when one of those young girls,

breastless and bred for the high bar and the horse,
    was flawless, and the cost

of excellence finally seemed to make sense,
    the applause unstoppable.

For a long time, I realized, nothing else
    had deeply touched me.

Beyond my terrace was the intimation of a path
    that led to a house

where a man, I imagined, would be praising
    his children, kissing his wife.

I could see myself just tapping that man
    with Chekhov's hammer,

letting in a little disease and poverty
    and heartbreak.

Three crows flew from one tree to another, speaking
    the controlled hysteria of crow,

and I made those small, necessary adjustments
    to keep them in focus.

I don't know why I wished they were cormorants
    and the trees pilings in a harbor,

or why I wanted to walk down my steps, clear-eyed,
    into the blur and the worry.

A Petty Thing

An early frost, and a lone cricket
rubbing his forelegs together, slowly now,
a minor, somewhat courageous sound
in my heartless room where I've come,
heavy-chested, to be alone.
I mean *heatless*, heartless was a slip,
a betrayal really, of the mind.
No doubt the mind wants it to stay.
The cricket reminds me of Eastern Europe,
some bewildered communist holding on.
Now the map-makers, bored for years,
have new squiggly lines to draw.
It's a good time to be Lithuanian—
the cricket has reminded me of this too—
and countless henchmen and torturers
are out of work. Should we feel sad
for their families? I can't decide.
In my heatless room I've been thinking
that the duty-before-pleasure people
balance the books for those of us
dutiful about our pleasures,
and how exemplary crickets are,
playing out their brief summers,
transcending ugliness with song.
The temperature is falling. Night already
has fallen, which is inexact.
Night has come laterally
out of the woods, has risen from the grass.
Everything shy about me loves it,
everything criminal too.
A very petty thing is troubling me,
like one sock missing, though this
is not about socks.
It's so petty I've just been overly polite,
used the famous lie words,

fine and yes and goodnight.
Nearby, I know, mice are squinching
themselves tiny, getting into homes.
They're making important nests
out of dust and hair.
That cricket and the persistent friction
of its rubbing will soon be gone.
It's a sexual song, isn't it,
that crickets sing? They do it to be heard.

Honesty

The pines were swaying in the serious wind
    and clouds moved
like white pleasure boats, toward another world.
    There was a drift
of disorder in the air. There was a hint
    of ruckus in the way
the rotting fenceposts kept absolutely still.
    Lucky no one I loved
was nearby; I felt an odd welling up,
    an honesty coming on.
A woodpecker was eating, broadcasting the news.
    You have to have style
to survive such attention to yourself.
    You have to look that good
standing perpendicular as you peck and thunk.
    The serious wind
yielded to the blank otherness of calm.
    I could hear cars
on the Interstate. I could smell my own skin.
    That woodpecker had wings.
After its meal, its noise, it didn't stay around.
    If there isn't a God
maybe there's just a sense we're not
    sufficiently large.
Maybe only through irreverence can we find
    our true size.
That's what I was thinking when my dog came
    carrying a stick.
He wanted to play. He shook his head and tightened
    his grip as if keeping
were fun, possibly generous. Deer were hiding
    in the underbrush.
Only their hungers would make them come out,
    and this wasn't the time,
it wasn't dusk and even the calm wasn't quiet enough.

Wind in a Jar

for Deborah Whitman

I had been thinking of Bosnians and Serbs,
another stupid slaughter in a world
I could not disavow as mine,
when in your studio you said
This is wind in a jar. I saw the white hint
of turbulence near the bottom
of an irregular rhombus—a jar
because you called it a jar—
and I could look right in at the fixed wind
and the mere air that surrounded it.
I was happy you had caught the wind,
which for centuries had been as reckless
as anyone angry and unattached,
happy you'd given it such a resting place.
I wanted you to make a jar
for certain dark sections of the heart,
and a jar for honesty that hurts,
and a jar open on all sides—a freedom jar—
that would hold only what wished to be held.
But I had to say goodbye, or once again get lost
in the flux and effluvia of life and art.
Outside in the warm unauthorized night,
a small breeze had come up, a fledgling wind,
something that had gotten away, I was sure,
from somewhere, and would roam
the torturous earth for as long as it could.

The Woman with Five Hearts

The woman with five hearts knew what she had,
knew what we lacked. She bet high and then
higher; it was what any of us would have done.
                    A woman with five hearts,
we concluded, was a dangerous thing.
She did not think it romantic, what she had.
    She knew it was better
than two pair, better than anything straight.
She was sure I, for example, had weakness,
three of something at best.
                    The man to my right
clearly resented the woman with five hearts.
He touched her arm, as if this were a different game.
He tried to be ironic, but instead was mean.
    The woman with five hearts saw him
as a man with clubs, one fewer than he needed.
A man without enough clubs can be a pathetic thing.
Each of her bets demanded he come clean.
                    It was simple prudence
to yield to such a woman, a woman with all that.
The rest of us did, understanding so many hearts
could not be beaten, not with what we had.
But the man to my right decided to bluff.
    He raised her with what seemed
his entire body, everything he had been and was.
The woman with five hearts raised back,
amused now, as if aware of an old act—
                    a man with nothing puffing himself up.
He stayed because by now it had all gone
too far, a woman with five hearts and a man
                    without enough clubs.
And when she showed him all five, beautifully red,
he had to admit that was exactly what she had.

Night Truths

I've known an edginess, come evening,
when I haven't chosen to be alone, but am,
the necessity of music, the implacable silence
of the telephone, when my faith is faith
in the provisional, wild, no consolation
in it, and deeply, late at night, in the
peaty, musk-scented, moon-driven dark
I've felt so singular,
so importantly sorry for myself,
or so exquisitely stilled, attuned,
that I knew there were night truths
unavailable to lovers or the loved,
thought I might be close to them,
and have put off sleep because sleep
is social, intrusive, all the uninvited
waiting to make their appearances, put it off
until it came for me, ignorantly, persuasive.

Something Like Happiness

Last night Joan Sutherland was nuancing
the stratosphere on my fine-tuned tape deck,
and there was my dog Buster with a flea rash,
his head in his privates. Even for Buster
this was something like happiness. Elsewhere
I knew what people were doing to other people,
the terrible hurts, the pleasures of hurting.
I repudiated Zen because it doesn't provide
for forgiveness, repudiated my friend X
who had gotten "in touch with his feelings,"
which were spiteful and aggressive. *Repudiate*
felt good in my mouth, like someone else's tongue
during the sweet combat of love.
I said out loud, *I repudiate,* adding words
like *sincerity, correctness, common sense.*
I remembered how tired I'd grown of mountaintops
and their thin, unheavenly air,
had grown tired, really, of how I spoke of them,
the exaggerated glamor, the false equation between
ascent and importance. I looked at the vase
and its one red flower, then the table
which Zennists would say existed
in its *thisness,* and realized how wrong it was
to reject appearances. How much more difficult
to accept them! I repudiated myself, citing my name.
The phone rang. It was my overly serious friend
from Syracuse saying *Foucault, Foucault,*
like some lost prayer of the tenured.
Advocates of revolution, I agreed with him, poor,
screwed for years, angry—who can begrudge them
weapons and victory? But people like us,
Joan Sutherland on our tapes and enough fine time
to enjoy her, I said, let's be careful
how we link thought and action,
careful about deaths we won't experience.

I repudiated him and Foucault, told him
that if Descartes were alive and wildly in love
he himself would repudiate his famous dictum.
I felt something like happiness when he hung up,
and Buster put his head on my lap,
and without admiration stared at me.
I would not repudiate Buster, not even his fleas.
How could I? Once a day, the flea travels
to the eye of the dog for a sip of water.
Imagine! The journey, the delicacy of the arrival.

Some Things I Wanted to Say to You

If the horse you ride
is blind it's good
that it also be slow,
and please stroke it
a hundred more times than you would
the powerful, dazzling one.

To be generous is one thing,
but there's a clerk in some of us,
quick to say yes.
Worry about the command
in the suggestion.
Worry about smiles, and those men
whose business is business.

There are the joys and enigmas
of an evening alone
to appreciate.
There are always the simple events
of your life
that you might try to convert
into legend.

Did you know
that a good dog in your house
can make you more thoughtful,
even more moral?

And sex without conversation,
sex that's exotic or sleepy . . .
oh don't let anybody tell you
there's a wrong way to have it.

Tell your lovers the world
robs us in so many ways

that a caress is your way
of taking something back.
Tell the dogs and the horses
you love them more than cars.
Speak to everything
would be my advice.

Moralists

Whenever I've been one, I've known the end
of my thinking in advance, the door shut
before it's opened wide enough to let in
the ill wind, the rude, spectacular visage,
the simple truth obstructed in a corner.
Yet there's an advantage to limitation,
if one doesn't make a career of it.
There's an advantage even to good behavior,
especially after a week, say, of redefining it.
Sometimes a bad thing has felt so good
I wouldn't let anyone name it for me
ever again. And what's moral
had a new gaiety to it, an exuberance,
and I walked through the dull streets
like someone ablaze from the inside,
as close as I'd ever be, could be, to God.

Decorum

She wrote, "They were making love
up against the gymnasium wall,"
and another young woman in class,
serious enough to smile, said

"No, that's fucking, they must
have been fucking," to which many
agreed, pleased to have the proper fit
of word with act.

But an older woman, a wife, a mother,
famous in the class for confusing grace
with decorum and carriage,
said the F-word would distract

the reader, sensationalize the poem.
"Why can't what they were doing
just as easily be called making love?"
It was an intelligent complaint,

and the class proceeded to debate
what's fucking, what's making love,
and the importance of context, tact,
the *bon mot*. I leaned toward those

who favored fucking; they were funnier
and seemed to have more experience
with the happy varieties of their subject.
But then a young man said, now believing

he had permission, "What's the difference,
you fuck 'em and you call it making love;
you tell 'em what they want to hear."
The class jeered, and another man said

"You're the kind of guy who gives fucking
a bad name," and I remembered how fuck
gets dirty as it moves reptilian
out of certain minds, certain mouths.

The young woman whose poem it was,
small-boned and small-voiced,
said she had no objection to fucking,
but these people were making love, it was

her poem and she herself up against
that gymnasium wall, and it felt like love,
and the hell with all of us.
There was silence. The class turned

to me, their teacher, who they hoped
could clarify, perhaps ease things.
I told them I disliked the word fucking
in a poem, but that fucking

might be right in this instance, yet
I was unsure now, I couldn't decide.
A tear formed and moved down
the poet's cheek. I said I was sure

only of "gymnasium," sure it was
the wrong choice, making the act seem
too public, more vulgar than she wished.
How about "boat house?" I said.

Beautiful Women

More things come to them,
and they have more to hide.
All around them: mirrors, eyes.
         In any case
they are different from other women
and like great athletes have trouble
making friends, and trusting a world
quick to praise.

I admit without shame
I'm talking about superficial beauty,
the beauty unmistakable
to the honest eye, which causes
some of us to pivot and to dream,
to tremble before we dial.

        Intelligence warmed by generosity
is inner beauty, and what's worse
some physically beautiful women have it,
and we have to be strapped and handcuffed
to the mast, or be ruined.

But I don't want to talk of inner beauty,
it's the correct way to talk
and I'd feel too good
about myself, like a parishioner.
        Now, in fact,
I feel like I'm talking
to a strange beautiful woman at a bar, I'm
animated, I'm wearing that little fixed
smile, I might say anything at all.

Still, it's better to treat a beautiful woman
as if she were normal, one of many.
She'll be impressed that you're unimpressed,

might start to lean your way.
This is especially true if she has aged
into beauty, for she will have learned
the sweet gestures one learns
in a lifetime of seeking love.
Lucky is the lover of such a woman
and lucky the woman herself.

Beautiful women who've been beautiful girls
are often in some tower of themselves
waiting for us to make the long climb.

But let us have sympathy for the loneliness
of beautiful women.
Let us have no contempt for their
immense privilege, or for the fact
that they never can be wholly ours.

                    It is not astonishing
when the scared little girl in all of them
says here I am, or when they weep.
But we are always astonished by what
beautiful women do.

"Boxers punch harder when women are around,"
Kenneth Patchen said. Think what happens
when *beautiful* women are around.
We do not question
that a thousand ships were launched.

In the eye of the beholder? A platitude.
A beautiful woman enters a room,
and everyone beholds. Geography changes.
We watch her everywhere she goes.

A Good Life

It was on evenings like this,
in spite of the good talk
and drink, no more love-worries
than usual, and a fine commotion
of crickets in the late summer heat,
it was on evenings like this he knew
his true life lay elsewhere, it must,
so much acceptable pleasure here
yet so much yearning. He was home,
some muted pinprick of unease
prodding him, dully, from afar.

He told a story about a black bear
who swam the Delaware Water Gap
to get to New Jersey, where bears
can't be hunted, a story of animal wisdom,
survival. As if the bear knew,
as if there were a secret network of bears.

His guests were pleased.

The state of Pennsylvania wanted its bear
returned. In fact, New Jersey owed them
nine bears, there was proof.
Like certain departures, betrayals,
it became a matter for the courts—
the rights of bears, of hunters and bureaucrats . . .

You can walk out of your life
if sadness properly instructs you.
And can't humiliation send you,
knees bleeding, over the forbidden wall?
That's what he was thinking
as his wife poured more wine for the guests,
as a beneficent moon half-lit the yard

and the erotics of friendship
made its edgy argument against despair.

The guests left; it was time.
He and his wife cleaned up, talked,
made sweet, drunken love.
Nothing was wrong. Nothing was wrong
except there was this life,
intuited, unclaimed.
He suspected she sensed it too, hers,
something more utterly hers.

Elsewhere bears were trusting their bodies
to take them to safety, but what did bears know
about water and wind and chance?
He could see a bear caught in turbulence,
swept downriver, where no law
could keep it from being killed.

It's a comedy, he thought.
His hand was resting on her hip,
it could be anybody's hip,
anybody's hand . . . In a dream
Stendhal heard Don Juan speak:
"There are not twenty different sorts of women,
and once you've had two or three of each sort,
boredom sets in." To which Stendhal said,

"A man who trembles is not bored."

Maybe it was all about trembling,
some old trepidation before the next step.
Maybe, like Stendhal, you connive
to give yourself a wake-up call
in the middle of the night.

He kissed her, and in the settled dark
rolled away into the other world
of their bed. It was easy.
   No, that was not applause
coming from the crickets.
He understood that relentless buzz, more
than mere desire, less than misery.

The Resurrection

In the converted stable where I work,
after the kerosene warmed the room,
one deadened fly rose to life—
a phenonemon that could turn a boy
from street crime to science
or, if less bright, to the church.
Lucky such a boy wasn't present.
I watched that fly push against the window
as if it had just learned something
about the locomotion of its wings
and its little fly heart. Perhaps
it wanted to foul whatever it could reach,
an act, no doubt, of temperament and taste.
I was beginning, no, deciding,
to be the poet of this fly, didn't every thing
in the world need its poet?
and I would tell of its resurrection
in a deceptive room with temporary heat
and illusory glass. To be a fly
was to fly in the face
of all that could defeat it,
and there was the pleasure of shit
to look forward to, the pleasure of bothering
cows and people, the pleasure of pure speed.
Another fly rose and pushed
against the window, two flies now,
and suddenly I was poet of flies in winter
as they sought the other side
of the glass, which was death,
victims of having once risen, ignorant
buggers, happy on bad evidence, warm, abuzz.

The Vanishings

One day it will vanish,
how you felt when you were overwhelmed
by her, soaping each other in the shower,
or when you heard the news
of his death, there in the T-Bone diner
on Queens Boulevard amid the shouts
of short-order cooks, Armenian, oblivious.
One day one thing and then a dear other
will blur and though they won't be lost
they won't mean as much,
that motorcycle ride on the dirt road
to the deserted beach near Cadiz,
the Guardia mistaking you for a drug-runner,
his machine gun in your belly—
already history now, merely *your* history,
which means everything to you.
You strain to bring back
your mother's full face and full body
before her illness, the arc and tenor
of family dinners, the mysteries
of radio, and Charlie Collins,
eight years old, inviting you
to his house to see the largest turd
that had ever come from him, unflushed.
One day there'll be almost nothing
except what you've written down,
then only what you've written down well,
then little of that.
The march on Washington in '68
where you hoped to change the world
and meet beautiful, sensitive women
is choreography now, cops on horses,
everyone backing off, stepping forward.
The exam you stole and put back unseen
has become one of your stories,

overtold, tainted with charm.
All of it, anyway, will go the way of icebergs
come summer, the small chunks floating
in the Adriatic until they're only water,
pure, and someone taking sad pride
that he can swim in it, numbly.
For you, though, loss, almost painless,
that Senior Prom at the Latin Quarter—
Count Basie and Sarah Vaughan, and you
just interested in your date's cleavage
and staying out all night at Jones Beach,
the small dune fires fueled by driftwood.
You can't remember a riff or a song,
and your date's a woman now, married,
has had sex as you have
some few thousand times, good sex
and forgettable sex, even boring sex,
oh you never could have imagined
back then with the waves crashing
what the body could erase.
It's vanishing as you speak, the soul-grit,
the story-fodder,
everything you retrieve is your past,
everything you let go
goes to memory's out-box, open on all sides,
in cahoots with thin air.
The jobs you didn't get vanish like scabs.
Her goodbye, causing the phone to slip
from your hand, doesn't hurt anymore,
too much doesn't hurt anymore,
not even that hint of your father, ghost-thumping
on your roof in Spain, hurts anymore.
You understand and therefore hate
because you hate the passivity of understanding
that your worst rage and finest

private gesture will flatten and collapse
into history, become invisible
like defeats inside houses. Then something happens
(it is happening) which won't vanish fast enough,
your voice fails, chokes to silence;
hurt (how could you have forgotten?) hurts.
Every other truth in the world, out of respect,
slides over, makes room for its superior.

Afterlife

There've been times I've thought worms
    might be beneficent, speeding up,
as they do, the dissolution of the body.

I've imagined myself streamlined, all bone
    and severity,
pure mind, free to contemplate the startling

absence of any useful metaphysics, any final
    punishment or reward.
Indulgences, no doubt. Romances I've allowed myself

when nothing ached, and the long diminishment
    seemed far off.
Today I want my body to keep making its sloppy

requests. I'm out among the wayward dazzle
    of the countryside,
which is its own afterlife, wild, repeatable.

There's no lesson in it for me. I just like
    its ignorant thrust,
its sure way back, after months without desire.

Are wildflowers holy? Are weeds?
    There's infinite hope
if both are, but perhaps not for us.

To skirt the woods, to walk deeply like this
    into the high grass,
is to invoke the phantasms of sense

and importance. I think I'm smelling the rain
    we can smell before it rains.
It's the odor of another world, I'm convinced,

and means nothing, yet here it is, and here
    sweetly it comes
from the gray sky into the small openings.

from

LOOKING FOR HOLES
IN THE CEILING (1974)

What

What starts things

are the accidents behind the eyes
touched off by, say, the missing cheekbone
of a woman who might have been beautiful

it is thinking about
your transplanted life-line going places
in someone else's palm, or the suicidal games
your mind plays with the edge
of old wounds, or something
you couldn't share with your lover

there are no endings

people die between birthdays and go on for years;
what stops things for a moment
are the words you've found for the last bit of light
you think there is

Teacher Answering Young Radicals

Given the choice of blowing up the Empire
State Building or a department store, he said balloons
took his breath away, too.

Then he took the wind in his fist
and let it out like a butterfly,
to show what power was.

When no one understood,
he let himself go
and they followed the simple flight of his mind

flower to flower. Then he raised his fist
into a hammer and slammed it to the table,
to show what weakness was.

He had them,
and could have lifted them with his voice
to where blood gets thin as air

and honest rage suffocates in the throat.
He told them instead about his fist,
the dull pain up his arm, turning warm.

Biography in the First Person

This is not the way I am.
Really, I am much taller in person,
the hairline I conceal reaches back
to my grandfather, and the shyness my wife
will not believe in has always been why
I was bold on first dates. All my uncles
were detectives. My father a crack salesman.
I've saved his pins, the small acclamations
I used to show my friends. And the billyclub
I keep by my bed was his, too; an heirloom.
I am somewhat older than you can tell.
The early deaths have decomposed
behind my eyes, leaving lines apparently caused
by smiling. My voice still reflects the time
I believed in prayer as a way of getting
what I wanted. I am none of my clothes.
My poems are approximately true.
The games I play and how I play them
are the arrows you should follow: they'll take you
to the enormous body of a child. It is not
that simple. At parties I have been known to remove
from the bookshelf the kind of book
that goes best with my beard.
My habits in bed are so perverse they differentiate me
from no one. And I prefer soda, the bubbles just after
it's opened, to anyone who just lies there. Be careful:
I would like to make you believe in me.
When I come home at night after teaching myself
to students, I want to search the phone book
for their numbers, call them, and pick their brains.
Oh, I am much less flamboyant than this.
If you ever meet me, I'll be the one with the lapel
                full of carnations.

From "Sympathetic Magic"

LOVERS

To keep the one you want
dig up a footprint of hers
and put it in a flowerpot.
Then plant a marigold, the flower
that doesn't fade.
And love her.
If she's distant now
it's for a reason beyond control.
So don't tamper with the impressions
left by her body when
for the last time
she leaves your bed.
Just smooth them out
and forget her.
Who is not vulnerable
to a stronger magic (the
broken glass, the bullets
in a yawn),
the terrible power of the one
less in love.

CHIPPING AWAY AT DEATH

Build a man of straw and rags
and give him a foolish, battered hat.
There, he is you in old age.
Then when the swallows come
from the south, dig up the brandy
you buried the year before.
Taste it. It will taste like
the musk of a religion
you gave up
for the sweeter taste of women.
Cover your straw man with it.

Light a match.
If you want to throw chestnuts
into the fire and sing
squalid songs as he burns, do so.
You are making sure none of this
will ever happen,
making sure this is one death
you will not suffer.

TRAVELING

If you travel alone, hitchhiking,
sleeping in woods,
make a cathedral of the moonlight
that reaches you, and lie down in it.
Shake a box of nails
at the night sounds
for there is comfort in your own noise.
And say out loud:
somebody at sunrise be distraught
for love of me,
somebody at sunset call my name.
There will soon be company.
But if the moon clouds over
you have to live with disapproval.
You are a traveler,
you know the open, hostile smiles
of those stuck in their lives.
Make a fire.
If the Devil sits down, offering companionship,
tell him you've always admired
his magnificent, false moves.
Then recite the list
of what you've learned to do without.
It is stronger than prayer.

Day and Night Handball

I think of corner shots, the ball
hitting and dying like a butterfly
on a windshield, shots so fine
and perverse they begin to live

alongside weekends of sex
in your memory. I think of serves
delivered deep to the left hand,
the ball sliding off the side wall

into the blindnesses of one's body,
and diving returns that are impossible
except on days when your body is all
rubber bands and dreams

unfulfilled since childhood.
I think of a hand slicing the face
of a ball, so much english
that it comes back drunk

to your opponent who doesn't have
enough hands to hit it,
who hits it anyway, who makes you think
of "God!" and "Goddamn!," the pleasure

of falling to your knees
for what is superb, better than you.
But it's position I think of most,
the easy slam and victory

because you have a sense of yourself
and the court, the sense that old men
gone in the knees have,
one step in place of five,

finesse in place of power,
and all the time
the four walls around you
creating the hardship, the infinite variety.

On Hearing the Airlines Will Use
a Psychological Profile to Catch
Potential Skyjackers

They will catch me
as sure as the check-out girls
in every Woolworths have caught me, the badge
of my imagined theft shining in their eyes.

I will be approaching the ticket counter
and knowing myself, myselves,
will effect the nonchalance of a baron.
That is what they'll be looking for.

I'll say "Certainly is nice that the
airlines are taking these precautions,"
and the man behind the counter
will press a secret button,

there'll be a hand on my shoulder
(this will have happened before in a dream),
and in a back room they'll ask me
"Why were you going to do it?"

I'll say "You wouldn't believe
I just wanted to get to Cleveland?"
"No," they'll say.
So I'll tell them everything,

the plot to get the Pulitzer Prize
in exchange for the airplane,
the bomb in my pencil,
heroin in the heel of my boot.

Inevitably, it'll be downtown for booking,
newsmen pumping me for deprivation
during childhood,
the essential cause.

"There is no one cause for any human act,"
I'll tell them, thinking *finally,*
a chance to let the public in
on the themes of great literature.

And on and on, celebrating myself, offering
no resistance, assuming what they assume,
knowing, in a sense, there is no such thing
as the wrong man.

How to Be Happy:
Another Memo to Myself

You start with your own body
then move outward, but not too far.
Never try to please a city, for example.
Nor will the easy intimacy
in small towns ever satisfy that need
you have only whispered in the dark.
A woman is a beginning.
She need not be pretty, but must know
how to make her own ceilings
out of all that's beautiful in her.
Together you must love to exchange
gifts in the night, and agree
on the superfluity of ribbons,
the fine violence of breaking out
of yourselves. No matter,
it's doubtful she will be enough for you,
or you for her. You must have friends
of both sexes. When you get together
you must feel everyone has brought
his fierce privacy with him
and is ready to share it. Prepare
yourself though to keep something back;
there's a center in you
you are simply a comedian
without. Beyond this, it's advisable
to have a skill. Learn how to make something:
food, a shoe box, a good day.
Remember, finally, there are few pleasures
that aren't as local as your fingertips.
Never go to Europe for a cathedral.
In large groups, create a corner
in the middle of a room.

from

FULL OF LUST
AND GOOD USAGE
(1976)

Beneath the Sidewalk

Whispers collect there, the bad news
from our subconscious,
tears that have dripped down
the inside of faces,
apologies that have gotten lost
in all of our throats.

So much has been held in,
so much has seeped through
the soles of our shoes,
that half our lives are beneath the sidewalk.
We sense the deep riot
that is always going on.

In spring there are small explosions.
Signs. This is why
the sidewalk must be repaved.
We hire someone to do it for us,
our tight bodies watching from windows.

Truck Stop: Minnesota

The waitress looks at my face
as if it were a small tip.
I'm tempted to come back at her
with *java*
but I say *coffee,* politely,
and tell her how I want it.
Her body has the alert sleepiness
of a cat's. Her face
the indecency of a billboard.
She is the America I would like to love.
Sweetheart, the truckers call her.
Honey. Doll.
For each of them, she smiles.
I envy them,
I'm full of lust and good usage,
lost here.
I imagine every man she's left with
has smelled of familiar food,
has peppered her with wild slang
until she was damp and loose.
I do nothing but ask for a check
and drift out into the night air—
let my dreams lift
her tired feet off the ground
into the sweet, inarticulate
democracy beyond my ears—
and keep moving until I'm home
in the middle of my country.

In the House

I am attracted by the dust
and silence of an upper shelf,
the strange air

that causes linoleum
to bulge in the cellar.
I know the walls come to hug

like grizzlies
if you stare at them too long,
and the kitchen knife

wants to be held.
I sense the aromas of sex,
the delicate, stale drift

of arguments and spite
no amount of cleaning will solve.
I know when love goes

it slips through all insulation,
forgets your name,
becomes sky.

One Side of the Story

I was thinking of
the candle and the candle's end
when you took your place at the table.
Of what to do when the words fail,
as they most surely will.
I was thinking
so many people walk up to me
and tell me they're dead,
though they're just describing their afternoons.
You had the black dress on
and through the candelabra
I could see the sad turn of your mouth.
I was thinking of ways
to keep the light going, of fires
larger than the house.
But when we spoke, remember? we spoke
about the passing of the food,
how the crumbs seem to collect on my side.

And nothing terrible happened that night,
and nothing since.
The candle I was thinking about
is simply gone, and the drippings gone,
scraped out of the holder.
The lights go out when we blow them out
or turn them off. It would be lovely,
wouldn't it? to think only what's been felt
remains: that black dress on the floor,
your skin and the drift of my hands.

Building in Nova Scotia

Before the grass could be planted
stones had to be picked
every day for a week
and then my wife took her urine somewhere
and in the evening she was pregnant
        it was a miracle
when the rocks were gone how the seed
took hold, changed,
if they had investigated her belly for prints
I would have been guilty, especially my lips
on the evening the news came—
the next day a tern, hunting for fish,
stopped in midair before it dove
        I tell you it was beautiful
how the sky gave way
to our house when it was finished
and the small imperialist in my body
gathered in the stars

A Romance

He called eel grass
what she called seaweed.
He insulated their house with it.
She was interested in
the transparence of her skin.
He walled the bathroom
with barn-siding, he built the couch
with wood he had chopped.
She, a friend once said,
was a calligrapher of the dark.
He dug a root cellar
to store vegetables. He built a shack
for his ducks. Once, while asleep,
he said "the half-shut eye of the moon."
She spoke about the possible
precision of doubt.
He knew when the wind changed
what weather it would bring.

She baked bread, made jam
from sugar berries, kept a notebook
with what she called
little collections of her breath.
He said the angle the nail goes in
is crucial.
She fed the ducks, called them
her sentient beings.
She wondered how one becomes
a casualty of desire.
He said a tin roof in summer
sends back the sun's heat.
She made wine from dandelions.
She once wrote in her notebook

"the ordinary loveliness of this world."
He built a bookcase
for her books.
They took long walks.

Those of Us Who
Think We Know

Those of us who think we know
the same secrets
are silent together most of the time,
for us there is eloquence
in desire, and for a while
when in love and exhausted
it's enough to nod like shy horses
and come together
in a quiet ceremony of tongues

it's in disappointment we look for words
to convince us
the spaces between stars are nothing
to worry about,
it's when those secrets burst
in that emptiness between our hearts
and the lumps in our throats.
And the words we find
are always insufficient, like love,
though they are often lovely
and all we have

Waiting with Two Members of a Motorcycle Gang for My Child to Be Born

for Andrea

I was talking to "The Eliminators"
   when you were born,
two of them, high as slag heaps and
   uncles to be,
all in black for the occasion.
   All you wanted was out;
you couldn't have known that you
   were "Life"
when you came, or that your father
   was let loose
from graduate school, a believer
   in symbols.
I expected "The Eliminators" to
   disappear, snuffed out
by a stronger force, a white tornado
   of my own.
That's not what happens, though,
   in life
as you will learn. They smiled when
   they heard of you
and shook my hand. At another time
   it might
have been my head. May you turn
   stone, my daughter,
into silk. May you make men better
   than they are.

For Fathers of Girls

for Susanne

When sperm leaves us
and we cockadoodledo
and our wives rise like morning

the children we start
are insignificant as bullets
that get lodged, say,

in a field somewhere
in the midwest.
If we are thinking then

it is probably of sleep
or the potency of rest, or
the one-hand catch we made

long ago at the peak of our lives.
Later, though, in a dream
we may imagine something in the womb

of our heads, neither boy nor girl,
nothing quite so simple.
But when we wake, our wives are

breathing like the wounded
on the whitest street in the world.
We are there

we are wearing conspicuous masks
for the first time,
our eyes show the sweat

from our palms.
Suddenly we are fathers
of girls: purply, covered with slime

we could kiss. There's a cry,
and the burden of living up
to ourselves is upon us again.

A Primer for Swimming
at Black Point

The bottom drops off quickly
and you're in over your head
among the crosscurrents,
the floating sea plants.
This is where to swim, though,
if you can, the water cold enough
to stir in you what's sleeping,
the fir trees on the other side
grand and achievable.
          Just think of your fear
as alertness, and be happy for it.
Without fear it's often tempting
to believe the water cares
about you; in its movement
your mother's voice.
Consider getting out then.
It will never tell you
this intimacy cannot go on.
          And when you get out
there'll be no evidence
you were ever in, just a
tingling, an aliveness
that hints insurrection
in the deepest parts of you,
and it too will pass.
Don't expect to know more
than your body has absorbed.

The Carpenter's Song

for Ted Porter

When I'm no longer young
let me be able to make wine
from chokecherries and care enough
to let it age. And when friends come
let them sip it
on a torn-out car seat under a tree.
And let my house smell of books
and pipe smoke, and let its disarray
be the luxury of a man
who makes cabinets.
And after it gets dark
let's move to the room
where the squeeze-box is, sing songs
and talk of Iceland by freighter,
Newfoundland on a whim, all the arrivals
one doesn't plan.
And let the evidence be deep
in my voice, the lines of my face.
And let me call this: style.

Let me rebuild then the lighthouse
my father rebuilt years ago,
and let me know the history
of old houses haunted by rats
and shadows, good people
and bad, and when asked
let me sense what can be redeemed
and what can't.
And yes, let me be able to say
I'm a builder of houses, a man
who works slow and knows
how hard it is
to get the inside just right.
And let my metaphors grow
from that, something lived stretching out

trying to make contact
with something else.
And let me call this: my work.

And when I'm no longer young
let there be poets in my life,
their words aftertastes on the tongue,
and let me speak those words like a man
who has heard a spar snap on a ship,
who has been lost once or twice
and come back.
And let me declare
I've been a lover of women
without declaring it, and feel
I've treated them better than wood,
knowing I've been a husband of wood,
have cared for it with my own hands.
And let my hands be thick
badges of power
rarely used, my fist an inner fist
the size of a heart,
and let this be visible to men.
And let the old deaf dog
sense me coming a long way off,
ready to forgive anything I've done—
and let me call all this: some goddamn luck.

Coming Home,
Garden State Parkway

Tonight the toll booth men are
congratulating the weather,
wishing me well. I'm all thank you's
and confusion, I don't know what

kind of conspiracy this is.
Then at Howard Johnson's
the pretty cashier apologizes
for the price of coffee. She wants me

to drive carefully, to think of her
on the dark, straight road.
Does she say these things to everyone?
I've done nothing different

and in the mirror
there's the same old face
not even lovers have called handsome,
the same mouth that belies

absolute conviction.
I'm alone, and maybe
there's an underworld of those alone
and maybe tonight I've entered it—

the instant, safe intimacy
guaranteed to move on.
On the car radio
comes a noisy current song

and then an old, melodic lie
about love.
Afterwards, the disc jockey
speaks to all of us on the road,

he wants us to understand
the danger of the other man,
watch out, he says, for the blind side.
I'm going 70, the winter outside

is without snow, it's hard anymore
to be sure about anything.
Next toll station, I feel for a quarter—
the exact change

but I swerve
(as I knew I would)
to the woman holding out her hand.
She neither smiles nor speaks;

I try to believe
she's shy.
I'd like to put my hand in her hand,
to keep alive

this strange human streak I'm on.
But there's only money between us,
silver and flesh
meeting in a familiar goodbye.

The Photograph Album

That is the face I wore
when such faces were being worn
and there is my body, desirous, hard,
its reflection in the lake—
boneless as a roll of skin.
This is the landscape I once believed
existed: small boats and a dark ridge
of pines to either side. Houses with docks.
The time my father's arm
was a wand.

It took years to learn
something always swims underwater
tugging at reflections, swallowing stones,
that my father could collapse from within
like any other man.
But those eyes,
the careful pendulum that grows behind them
as knowledge grows! Could they ever be
so open again?

Page after page, it's the same—
I was the boy who smiled too much,
the man who wished to be contained.
Even now a part of me is waiting
in the sunlight somewhere.

How to fill the blank pages?
I turn them and like a desert they seem
to demand nothing less than my bones—
photographs of places I may not come back from,
fingernails testing the borders,
blood or what's left over from love
in the margins.

from

A Circus
of Needs
(1978)

Midnight

Midnight in some midnight place.
And here the welcome dark
after a good day, the slight discomfort
of the six o'clock news.
In certain places midnight accumulates
at the end of a beggar's wrists:
ask for the time
and that's what time it is.
What can I do but laugh
when I light a small lamp
in the basement and my daughter complains
"You put the light on
too dark down there."
She's always asleep at midnight,
she wakes in a bed surrounded
by posters of kittens.
Someday I'll have to tell her privilege
is what gets taken away.
People deep in midnight,
that's all they think about—
taking it away.
I'll have to tell her that.
On TV the other night
the South Bronx had no life
I could recognize.
The larvae of thieves in the gutters.
A small apocalypse.
Someday I'll have to tell my daughter
about the Bronx
before she walks through it,
though the Bronx might be everywhere
by then.
Here, the crocuses are coming up
and there are kittens by her bed.
This loveliness is hers by birth.

If I bring her up right
she'll hate that fact in a few years.
Is that true? Well, then
the people born into midnight—
they'll hate it for her.

The Man Who Never Loses His Balance

He walks the high wire in his sleep.
The tent is blue, it is perpetual
afternoon. He is walking between
the open legs of his mother
and the grave. Always. The audience
is fathers whose kites are lost, children
who want to be terrified into joy.
He is so high above them, so capable
(with a single, calculated move)
of making them care for him
that he's sick of the risks
he never really takes.
Every performance, deep down,
he tries one real plunge
off to the side, where the net ends.
The tent is blue. Outside is a world
that is blue. Inside him
a blueness that could crack
like china if he ever hit bottom.

Belly Dancer at the Hotel Jerome

Disguised as an Arab, the bouzouki player
introduces her as Fatima, but she's blond,
midwestern, learned to move we suspect
in Continuing Education, Tuesdays, some hip
college town.
We're ready to laugh, this is Aspen
Colorado, cocaine and blue valium
the local hard liquor, and we
with snifters of Metaxa in our hands,
part of the incongruous
that passes for harmony here.
But she's good. When she lets her hair loose,
beautiful. So we revise:
summer vacations, perhaps, in Morocco
or an Egyptian lover, or both.
This much we know:
no Protestant has moved like this
since the flames stopped licking their ankles.
Men rise from dinner tables
to stick dollar bills where their eyes
have been. One slips a five
in her cleavage. When she gets to us
she's dangling money
with a carelessness so vast
it's art, something perfected, all her bones
floating in milk.
The fake Arabs on bongos and bouzouki are real
musicians, urging her, whispering
"Fatima, Fatima," into the mike
and it's true, she has danced the mockery out
of that wrong name in this unlikely place,
she's Fatima and the cheap, conspicuous dreams
are ours, rising now, as bravos.

Sister

The sister I never had
enters my wife when I am
sleeping next to her.
So many times
I've watched my sister
come from her separate room,
the room that long ago
in a house of brothers
was an extra room
down the hall from where
I would dream her alive.
She climbs into bed
on my wife's side
and I touch my wife awake
for now my sister and she
are the woman I must talk to
about incompleteness and love.
Awake, she doesn't know
my sister is in her,
she doesn't know why my embrace
has so much gratefulness in it,
why my questions are all
whispered as if
a father could overhear us.
She thinks I want to
make love but I remove
her hand and hold it,
ask another question
about high school and loss,
the kind of loss
that repeats itself every day
like being born
without a leg.
I watch my sister leave
as my wife takes me

in her arms, says hush,
you've been talking again,
sleep now,
and I curl into her
as if it were possible
she could be everything to me,
alone like this,
just ourselves.

Here and There

Here and there nightfall
without fanfare
presses down, utterly
expected, not an omen in sight.
Here and there a husband
at the usual time
goes to bed with his wife
and doesn't dream of other women.
Occasionally a terrible sigh
is heard, the kind that is
theatrical, to be ignored.
Or a car backfires
and reminds us of a car
backfiring, not of a gunshot.
Here and there a man says
what he means and people hear him
and are not confused.
Here and there a missing teenage girl
comes home unscarred.
Sometimes dawn just brings another
day, full of minor
pleasures and small complaints.
And when the newspaper arrives
with the world,
people make kindling of it
and sit together while it burns.

Split: 1962

You hold the negative up
to the light, appreciating the shadows.
It is you and I posing
as you and I, what seems coming apart
at the seam at some hidden locus,
some meeting place of sensation and nerve.
Looking at ourselves this way
we are surrounded by the low clouds
of trees in full bloom, my hand in yours
is an erasure, perfect, oracular.

Now you take the scissors and cut me
out, keeping me for yourself.
Then you hand me
you. The sentimental we agree
has its place, if undeveloped.
I place you in my wallet
in the compartment I never use
so the light cannot touch you.
You do the same, as if it were possible
nothing could ruin us now—
so separate, almost unborn again.

Essay on Sanity

I am tired of hearing the insane
   lauded for their clear
      thinking. If they do

get to the reddest heart of things
   it's because they can't see
      the world of appearances,

where you are, struggling to separate
   the difficult jewel from the
      chalcedony that surrounds it.

And I love the world
   of appearances with its blue veils,
      its bright tintinnabulations, I

wouldn't give it up for that dark laser
   the mad point
      in no special direction.

(Except, of course,
   for an afternoon of white light
      with you somewhere.)

The point is you, who romanticize
   those who are wise and sad
      and tortured, *you* wouldn't

want to be *them*. And, sure,
   we are sad too in our daily indifference
      to the moon inside us, in

our sleeping bodies, but there is
   a difference—it is, say,
      having breakfast with someone

you love, the calm small ordinary
   exchanges between people
      who know knives

every once in a while are *not*
   the silvercoated castrati
      of their worst dreams. People who

can read a book or newspaper, play
   ball or attend an orgy, who can do
      all these without carrying around

a picture of that cracked ceiling and its
   one enormous spider, who can do
      everything without the fear

that their heads can be entered
   by a dark god, a terrible
      flickering clarity.

Let us not romanticize them! They
   who can't return to the small talk
      of any given evening.

Who is sane is a question
   of resistance, the mind saying No
      to the sanctioned lies, the body

speaking up to the inner ear
   that has been educated to hear it.
      It is a question

of moments; people in the first rush
   of love are the most sane,
      the most able to feel their way

into importance. When the sign says
    Underarm Deodorants, they will put
        their tongues into each other's

armpits. When someone publishes a treatise
    on love, theirs will be the pantomime
        that mocks it—just as

the truly sane person will mock
    this poem by simply walking
        into any room!

Nevertheless it is with our poems
    that we must visit ourselves, who are
        neither here

nor there. And those never astonished
    by their own humanity, smack
        in the arid middle.

But I am tired of insanity
    being attributed to the middle
        class. Even *they* know the real issue

is lack of courage, a standing still
    while the distant children
        of their desires cry out

from a burning building. Insight
    is the awful burden. They know this.
        To be sane, perhaps, is to bring it

to the magnificent thin-as-ice world
    of appearances, making sure the rope
        that keeps you from the abyss

is secured around your waist,
　　so you're free enough
　　　　to know everything superficial

is as real as that which
　　it conceals. The mad, those who
　　　　are so beautiful

when years later we read what they said,
　　reject the smile for the teeth
　　　　behind it, cannot help

themselves, remind us always,
　　like conscience, they are
　　　　terrible companions.

Introduction to the 20th Century

The conveyor belts bearing hubcaps and loneliness
were everywhere, and the invisible ruts in the air
could transport you for a lifetime
if you weren't careful. Monotony had a hair trigger
and there were machines that sounded like the sea
and put you to sleep if the jackhammers were thumping.
Oh, when the sun broke through the pink haze
of our luxuries, lovers were seen falling into the same
ancient swoon. And the ledgers of motels
grew spectacular with aliases, there was no way
to escape the Day-Glo and boldface, the suburbs
crowded with manuals.

Yet some of us were happy for hours, days, weeks.
Even in the subways there were people to love,
there were children who ripped apart their mothers
to get into the world, and the mothers called them
Daughter or Son, and the fathers got drunk
and felt they had a say in the universe.
This would happen every day! And for every death
there was a building or a poem. For every
lame god a rhythm and a hunch, something local
we could possibly trust. We learned to put
history books down gently on the table,
conscious of the Hitlers in them, the Stalins,
monsters that were ours and no one else's.
In difficult times, we came to understand,
it's the personal and only the personal that matters.

This Late in the Century

I walk the streets
always a gesture away from contact,
ungiven gifts, first words
it would seem foolish to say.

And then I forget about it all
and go about my half-desired loneliness,
back to the body's asylum
way back here where the movie

of the world is playing and all of us
are watching one seat apart.
Sometimes even after I return home
the stranger I am

will find those pockets
of collapsed air
where not even kisses
can find him. Other times

I watch any two of us
form the modern we
out of our separate lives;
I bring my distances, say,

to yours, you bring yours to mine,
and with such safety
the first words, the lovely intimate
incomplete sentence.

Danse Manhattanique

Let us know each other by this
dance, barefoot, over bits of glass.
Let our arms
discover what's in the air
around us, how much resistance,
what passages, our fingertips alive
to high frequencies, doubts, jazz.
Let's move
to the jugular pulse of our lives,
shake our asses
to the sound of petty crime,
a cash register opening,
a libido humming
in a nearby room.
And when we return to our chairs,
the dance floor
arid with our absence,
let's invent the brawl
that starts at the bar—two men, say,
who need the exercise,
let's conjure the bloodbeat,
the contagion of violence,
and slip out into the street
with such things behind us,
having done and survived them.
Let's then (for a moment,
in our minds) take the Thruway upstate
and arrive at a place
where good days slide so easily
into the bad they deprive us
of grand gestures.
Let there be trees. Vacancies
for belief. The sky, perhaps,
as it once was.

Fable of the Water Merchants

One day the water merchants came
to town, saying "Let the water pass
over our hands, it will taste better."
And the people agreed and became addicted
     to that taste.
Then the water merchants threatened
to take away their hands, and the people
brought seed and chickens and placed them
     at their feet.
But already the water merchants had carved
replicas of their hands out of wood
and secured them to the river bank.
     The people said
"The water tastes different now"
and the water merchants replied "What you
are tasting, friends, is progress,"
and the people began to love it
and gave the merchants everything they wanted.

In a Dream of Horses

I think I loved the palomino best,
though the roan had the shoulders
of a horse that went wire to wire
for me once. This time
just some sleepy motion
around the moon, while the stars watched.
The night gave way
to the horses and kept on
closing up behind them. After a while
I was on the palomino. It was a race
for who could go slowest and yet
not break stride. Within the dream
I remember dreaming the postponement
of dawn, and promptly woke
as if I had broken some rule.
You were awake beside me
and in the retelling I put you
on the roan and added a forest,
feeling you wouldn't believe
I'd be riding alone in a dream,
in a dream of such obvious charm,
if I could help it.

The Worrier

So he wouldn't think of his children
he kept ordinary things around him,
things that wouldn't fail
or if they would, would not
be wept over: buck-ninety-five
dime novels, a black and white
television, nothing
so lamentable as children.
Even the most extraordinary of children,
which his were not, would fail
some false dream you had for them.
They would grow pubic hair and desires
no father could ignore
or do anything about—
no, he wanted nothing nearby
as lamentable as children or lap dogs
or even big dogs who curl
near your feet who die like parents
just when you've learned to live with them.
He liked things that were guaranteed—
the stereo's diamond needle, stoneware
plates, he would have liked classics
if he had known their definition.
These were not ordinary,
but ordinary comforts, dull after a while
like the perfectly insured body
of an athlete.
And that was how he wanted it
in his landscape of wishes.
All his children had been kidnapped
and hit by cars, oh so many times,
and still they came down each morning
from their bedrooms, incarnations of themselves,
bearing their lovely, intolerable futures
and the dog whined for food

and it was ghostly to live like this, he felt,
if only the dog were a teakettle
singing that it was ready,
if only his children
were somebody else's, unlovable,
whose funerals he might go to
out of some vague sense of duty.

Instead of You

I place a dead butterfly on the page,
this is called starting
with an image from real life.
It is gold and black
and, as if in some embalmer's dream,
a dusting of talc on its wings.
I have plans
for these wings. I will not let them
slip through my hands.
And if anyone is worried about how
the butterfly died, I'll tell them
my cat swatted it out of the air,
I just picked it up
and brought it to this page
with a notion of breathing
a different life into it. And I confess:
the cat's gesture was more innocent than mine.

The wings suggest nothing I want,
they are so lovely
I simply like the way they distract,
how my eye turns away from the living-
room, and the mind spins
into the silliness of spring.
I don't want much.
Just for certain private places
to remain open to me, that's all.
But this is no time to get ethereal.
Already, in a far corner of the page,
something dark is tempting me
to pull it into the poem. One tug
and it's a bat
trapped in sunlight, rabid with fear.

There's no way to keep the ugliness out,
ever. Drops of blood

beautiful, say, on the snow,
always lead to a wound.
Can this still turn out to be a love poem?
Can I still pull you from the wreckage
and kiss your bruises, so black and gold?
Is it too late to introduce you
who were always here, the watermark,
the poem's secret?
From the start all I wanted to explain
was how things go wrong,
how the heart's an empty place
until it is filled,
and how the darkness is forever waiting
for its chance.
If I have failed, know that I was trying
to get to you in my own way,
know that my cat never swatted a butterfly,
it was I who invented and killed it,
something to talk about
instead of you.

from

WORK AND LOVE

(1981)

Welcome

If you believe nothing is always what's left
after a while, as I did,
If you believe you have this collection
of ungiven gifts, as I do (right here
behind the silence and the averted eyes)
If you believe an afternoon can collapse
into strange privacies—
how in your backyard, for example,
the shyness of flowers can be suddenly
overwhelming, and in the distance
the clear goddamn of thunder
personal, like a voice,
 If you believe there's no correct response
to death, as I do; that even in grief
(where I've sat making plans)
there are small corners of joy
If your body sometimes is a light switch
in a house of insomniacs
If you can feel yourself straining
to be yourself every waking minute
If, as I am, you are almost smiling . . .

Checklist

The housework, the factory work, the work
that takes from the body
and does not put back.
The white-collar work and the dirt
of its profits, the terrible politeness
of the office worker, the work that robs
the viscera to pay the cool
surfaces of the brain. All the work
that makes love difficult, brings on
sleep, drops the body off
at the liquor cabinet. All the work
that reaches the intestines and sprawls.
And the compulsive work after the work
is done, those unfillable spaces
of the Calvinist, or certain marriage beds.

My Brother's Work

My brother who knows
the indignity of work
rides home with the taste of it
turning peptic, that odor
of swallowed pride rising
into his breath, his wife waiting
for the kiss that's so full
of the day she can't bear it.
My brother who hears the shout
of bosses, who is no boss himself,
only shouts at home,
thinks shouting is what permits
the bosses to move
with the easy self–
fulfilled gait of leopards
who've eaten all they've killed.
My brother who will not leave
his job wonders how Gauguin left
the world and found himself
on the other side of it.
"What *balls*," he says, "braver
than a suicide." My brother
who is no less than anyone
circumstance has made
to do its bidding, who wants
to rise one morning against
all odds and slip
into his leopard body,
my brother is
coming home now and his wife
is waiting for the kiss.

Hard Work
1956

At the Coke plant, toting empties
in large crates to the assembly line,
I envied my friends away at camp,
but the money was good
and hard work, my father said,
was how you became a man.
I saw a man for no special reason
piss into a Coke bottle
and put it back onto the line.
After a while I, too, hated
the bottles enough to break some
deliberately, and smile
and share with the other workers
a petty act of free will.
When I came home at night my body
hurt with that righteous hurt
men have brought home for centuries,
the hurt that demands
food and solicitation, that makes men
separate, lost.
I quit before the summer was over,
exercised the prerogatives of my class
by playing ball all August
and spent the money I'd earned
on Barbara Winokur, who was beautiful.
And now I think my job
must be phased out, a machine must
do it, though someone for sure
still does the hard work of boredom
and that person can't escape,
goes there each morning
and comes home each night
and probably has no opportunity
to say who he is

through destruction, some big
mechanical eye watching him
or some time and motion man
or just something hesitant, some father
or husband, in himself.

Workers

I've seen bees, in the spell of a queen,
mine the clover all afternoon
and ants, those laborers, hauling crumbs
to their elaborate dwellings
and lazy crows waiting
for something to be hit by a car
so the pickings will be easy.
And knowing they have no choice
but to obey the imperatives
of their natures, I've moved on
without judgment to the flies
born to be pests and the purple martins
that eat them, and I've been amazed
by the intelligence behind such work,
what eats what, and how much,
the incredible deathwork that is
the life of the universe.

And I've known the human-work
that uplifts and cleanses, glassblowers
as miraculous as seeds
which hold the shape of flowers,
ordinary people who rival the ant,
who call forth in emergencies
the cockroach's genius for survival.
And I've seen the crow-people too,
the sloth-people, the hyenas,
have seen the cruelty of nature
and the cruelty of economics
merge and twist into confusion,
and have marveled at the skunk
and its gorgeous white stripe
and its stink and have wondered
if the outlaw, in the company of outlaws,
planning his next job,
isn't the happiest man alive.

A Worker's Creed

From sunlight, the obvious and the lush.
The pleasures of exposure
and the pleasures of covering up
with a straw, broad-brimmed hat.
But I like cloudy days like this
after days like that.
Days I can gather speed
and open my eyes the whole way.
I like images like occluded front,
the aesthetics of sensing my shadow
lost in its own substance.
And I like the inspiration I get
from a sudden coolness,
days I can imagine Icarus thinking
"Not today," then doing
a little more work on his wings.

The Photograph in the Hallway

for D., "through with love"

You've seen it perhaps in the wrong setting,
a photograph of lovers in a haze
of abandon, everything in the room
background to their special dance.
Lacking nothing else,
what they seem to need is oxygen,
though this is the emergency
all of us try to arrive at,
equally breathless and contorted.

We've named it
"Mutual Generosity," two people
stopped in the equipoise
outside of time.
We're not deceived by such bliss;
the lovers have long ago returned
to the difficulties of loving.
Theirs is a moving picture now
subject to cool, inexorable laws.

But to say so is a pettiness.
Let us celebrate the photograph
as it is, which is as it might be
for you, after some straight line
in your life gives way
and luck is there like a net.
Let us stop and imagine it,
our fingers palpitating
as if their tips were missing—
such homelessness and longing in them,
such a desire to be properly lost.

The Clarities

The clarities at dusk, the ones
a lover pulling the shade knows

before he turns to face the imprecision
of a human face. The street light

coming on, the revelation of brown
as the color of melancholy, and melancholy

the mood that wants visitors
but will settle for the repetition

of a song. Now he turns
and sees her as she might have been

had she had less of this, a little more
of that, what light there is

is enough for the surgery that takes place
at the end of day, or love.

On the street below, traffic building up.
Somewhere an alibi fusing with a wish.

Meditation on Two Themes

1. The setting for joy is rarely
   where it occurs. That real place,
   that bed or playing field, is where
   we're stunned and the body is
   all fog and disbelief
   and we're making animal sounds
   or a new kind of silence.
   I remember feeling it
   afterwards driving home or
   the next day waking with it
   like sunlight on my face.
   I remember calling it joy
   over the phone, collecting it
   into a single word.

2. Suffering: we all know stories
   worse than our own.
   But I knew a good place for it—
   in the space between two garages,
   hidden by bushes.
   I was a child then, and once
   I stayed there an entire day and night.
   I was in pajamas, weeping.
   Before long
   I knew how much they'd miss me,
   how happy I could make them.

3. Last week the wife of a friend
   threw her baby out the window,
   proving that all settings are wrong
   if we are wrong or lost or crazy.
   For her there is no hiding,
   no place to run to.
   Across the street, the park
   is full of skaters.

Balloons rise above the trees
and wind, without rudder,
is once again king.

4. The sky won't stay still;
   this must account
   for its history of blueness.
   I know,
   I've followed a lone scud
   going nowhere at dusk
   and become that scud.
   I've pursued things
   long after they were over.
   Always I wanted someone
   to stop me.
   Isn't joy a kind of stillness
   at the top of something,
   before the long falling?

That Saturday Without a Car

for Ellen Dunn (1910–1969)

Five miles to my mother's house,
a distance I'd never run.
"I *think* she's dead"
my brother said, and hung up

as if with death
language should be mercifully approximate,
should keep the fact
that would forever be fact

at bay. I understood,
and as I ran wondered what words
I might say, and to whom.
I saw myself opening the door—

my brother, both of us, embarrassed
by the sudden intimacy we'd feel.
We had expected it
but we'd expected it every year

for ten: her heart was the best
and worst of her—every kindness
fought its way through damage,
her breasts disappeared

as if the heart itself, for comfort,
had sucked them in.
And I was running better
than I ever had. How different it was

from driving, the way I'd gone
to other deaths—
my body fighting it all off, my heart,
this adequate heart, getting me there.

Something

A wish for something moral like a wound
pitying the knife
its inability to be pleased or sad.
Or perhaps an afternoon one day a month
when everyone can say why they're ashamed.
Something to end the talk that passes
for talk. Something the lonesome ear,
the starved eye, can take in
like nourishment from the other world
in which, now and then, we've lived.

With No Experience in Such Matters

To hold a damaged sparrow
under water until you feel it die
is to know a small something
about the mind; how, for example,
it blames the cat for the original crime,
how it wants praise for its better side.

And yet it's as human
as pulling the plug on your Dad
whose world has turned
to feces and fog, human as . . .
well, let's admit, it's a mild thing
as human things go.

But I felt the one good wing
flutter in my palm—
the smallest protest, if that's what it was,
I ever felt or heard.
Reminded me how my eyelid has twitched,
the need to account for it.
Hard to believe no one notices.

Having Lost All Capacity

I am a man and count
nothing human alien to me.
                    —*Terence*

Today I read how Japanese fishermen
lured thousands of dolphins ashore,
slaughtering them because they eat fish
the fishermen want to catch and sell,
and tomorrow it'll be people once again
mutilating other people, and there'll come a time
when I'll just sit there turning the pages
having lost all capacity for horror
and so much that is human
will be alien to me I'll want to kill
all the killers, I'll walk past my wife
with a kitchen knife and out the door
into streets where others like me
will be slashing at wind and shadows . . .
until the first ripped neck.

I hear everything gets calmer then.
After the first time with a girl I remember
smelling my fingers and then tasting them,
and that's what I hear the first righteous
murder smells and tastes like, only better,
and with the headlines from a week of tabloids
in my mouth I'll know what the end
of the world tastes like, *irresistible,*
and that's all I can think about
here in my room, the sons of bitches,
the bastards!

Letter About Myself to You

to Joe Gillon, age 35,
four weeks to live

Joe,
the other day I tried to get my class
to believe something Keatsian and beautiful
about death. What scholastic rot,
true on cool days far away
from the latest personal taste of it.
Next time photos of Dachau, a little
real blood between the lines.
I used to believe in words, how they could
come together happily, and change.
Now I just pray they don't distort.
Cancer's my sign. See what I mean?
I just wanted to say *cancer*
the way a boy first says shit
in front of his parents. There, it's out.
Listen, I'm four years older than you
with a tennis date at five.
That's not guilt, it's another broken piece
among the puzzle's broken pieces,
it's the silence that comes back
after "Why?" is shouted in an empty room.
I need to know if love's absurd
to you now. Or meaningful, perhaps,
for the first time? Your wife,
do you want to make love to her,
or to everyone else? Do the ethics
of it matter, now, at all?
I need to know if rage helps,
if it feels good to spit
in an invisible eye? If resignation
is as sweet as sitting back
in a Jacuzzi with a telephone
and someone due to call?
Here, two thousand miles away,
I feel a tick in my cells;

you've brought out a selfishness, Joe,
please believe is empathy.
I'm writing this in the afternoon,
that time of day I'm most lost.
A wind is blowing insignificantly.
My cat, Peaches, curls on my lap,
humming like an extra heart.
What good are words?
I'm feeling that impotence which wants
a Lazarus to rise
everytime someone loved is sinking.
Rise. Miracle. Heaven.
There, I've said them, sadly,
to make you laugh.

Because We Are Not
Taken Seriously

Some night I wish they'd knock
on my door, the government men,
looking for the poem of simple truths
recited and whispered among the people.
And when all I give them is silence
and my children are exiled
to the mountains, my wife forced
to renounce me in public,
I'll be the American poet
whose loneliness, finally, is relevant,
whose slightest movement
ripples cross-country.

And when the revolution frees me,
its leaders wanting me to become
"Poet of the Revolution," I'll refuse
and keep a list of their terrible reprisals
and all the dark things I love
which they will abolish.
With the ghost of Mandelstam
on one shoulder, Lorca on the other,
I'll write the next poem, the one
that will ask only to be believed
once it's in the air, singing.

After Losses

for J.P.

Around the time the livingroom
became unbearable to look at
I took in two cats, a gray and a gray.
It was after the dog died and
the house was getting smaller.
It was after I rowed the small boat
into the seascape on the wall;
after I invented the small boat.
The cats ended all of that, for a while.
I was happy to watch them,
their speed and lassitude,
how when they were asleep
I could touch them awake.

But I began to hear the ho-hum
in each purr. I was witness
to the energy that misplaces itself
until it's gone. Mine, not theirs.
My dream: lying back
with a superficial wound, every hour
a nurse's breast glancing my arm.
Such a nice passivity that finally isn't
a life. Circles everywhere
looked like zeros to me.

I write this for you
who are surrounded by it now, the stasis
that won't end, these afternoons when
there's nothing to say
and you say it
in order to survive.
I want to tell you it ends,
it just goes away.
I remember a twitch in a vein—
as if something lost were tapping on a wall—

no, it wasn't that mystical.
I remember something like joy
coming with a fat pillow of its own . . .
no, it ends,
it just goes away.

Temporarily

The good, true enough stories
about the gods were gone forever—
the universe now was blue and invisible
and at night the stars
little more than a habit.
So when I woke and dressed

and walked out into the morning
I pretended the street rose up
to meet me. I met the facades,
the familiar hazards, eye-level.
Someone slim in knee boots
reminded me of the sexual collision

which for a moment or two
changes the world.
But a sign on a gas pump
cut to the heart:
"Temporarily out of Supreme."
Later, I saw my colleagues

carrying volumes
of Nietzsche and Marx, their bodies
looking as if they couldn't uphold
some colossal news.
And the students waiting in classrooms
for some utterly practical

invitation to the moon.
And me? From a mountaintop
a man with a telescope might have said,
"His day was daylight,
office-light, dusk and dark."
I walked out into the streets again,

the sure sanity of lovers
here and there. What did it matter
that I had the shards of a song
almost put together? It was so private
so full of the present
it would elevate nothing, cheer no one.

Fairy Tale

There was a small house that existed
and a wing to that house which didn't.
And he had made promises
about space and had once said
something about privacy, which everyone
in the house understood to be their own.
But the wing was not just a wing,
it needed a foundation and a roof
and most of all it needed money
so he told them wings are for the rich,
there would be no wing this year.
This was when the children wept
and reminded him of his promises,
and his wife said she couldn't live
without a wing, a wing was what
she dreamed of those nights
when the house was so small around her.
So his wife took a terrible job
typing the afterthoughts of those
with many wings, and the money
was green and full of plaster
and beams and so many windows.
That was how the wing the children
call their own was built and how
the distances in the house grew larger.
He sits in his room now,
the one on the other side of the house,
and his wife sits in her room
and there are hardly any accusations.

Amidst the Faltering

After a sentence by Galsworthy

Amidst the faltering and the falling apart
a ship goes down, my child's ship
in the bathtub, and the world seems silly again,
all the blossoms of doom I've imagined
reveal themselves as language, nothing more,
disconnected from this oddly nice day
I find myself in,
why even the sun is almost shining!

And the woman I love with all
the normal difficulties is suddenly naked
and her hair is wet and she's twisting
the water out of it. This, after bad blood
between us, another end of the world.
The muscles in her thin arms
are young peasants shifting in church.
Her breasts, those droplets on them,
could have been stolen
from one of Cezanne's bowls of fruit.

Maybe I've finally arrived at that high plateau
where philosophy lives with despair,
where nothing can be done but know
nothing can be done.
Maybe that's why I'm laughing,
why I feel like saying Jesus Christ
over and over again, as if it were a mantra
full of amazement and resignation.

I Come Home Wanting to Touch Everyone

The dogs greet me, I descend
into their world of fur and tongues
and then my wife and I embrace
as if we'd just closed the door
in a motel, our two girls slip in
between us and we're all saying
each other's names and the dogs
Buster and Sundown are on their hind legs,
people-style, seeking more love.
I've come home wanting to touch
everyone, everything; usually I turn
the key and they're all lost
in food or homework, even the dogs
are preoccupied with themselves,
I desire only to ease
back in, the mail, a drink,
but tonight the body-hungers have sent out
their long-range signals
or love itself has risen
from its squalor of neglect.
Everytime the kids turn their backs
I touch my wife's breasts
and when she checks the dinner
the unfriendly cat on the dishwasher
wants to rub heads, starts to speak
with his little motor and violin—
everything, everyone is intelligible
in the language of touch,
and we sit down to dinner inarticulate
as blood, all difficulties postponed
because the weather is so good.

To a Friend in Love with the Wrong Man Again

It was never meant to be sensible,
fully understandable. The digger wasp,
for example, goes up to the tarantula
like a friend and the tarantula freezes,
allows itself to be inspected.
Then it digs the tarantula's grave
while the tarantula watches. You, I bet,
would have guessed with a name
like *tarantula,* the tarantula would've been
the villain. But it is we who named
the tarantula and made the digger wasp
sound honest, hard-working.
And, of course, there is no villain,
only the scheme of things, only horror,
and occasionally the strange birth
of a butterfly and its short, gorgeous,
utterly careless season.
I should have mentioned the digger wasp
doesn't kill its victim, but stuns it,
drags it to the grave, lays one egg
on its stomach, and closes up.
You see, the instinct is maternal.
The newborn wasp feeds
off the tarantula for weeks,
digs itself out at the right time
and enters the odd, wonderful world.
I've no advice for you, my friend.
You, who would take it—
as all of us would—and offer it
up to the heart, like a sacrifice.

The Bad Angels

They are writing our names in the sky,
the bad angels with their calamitous wings.
They are spelling them wrong, exaggerating
the loops so that we'll see each other
askew, imperfect, like clouds broken off
from other clouds, separated by blue.

Worst part of me, old underminer
whom I've exiled unsuccessfully
into the far-away charged air,
I know it's your black-winged gang.
I wish I had some invisible means
of support, some magic against you.
I wish I could marshall all
that's ever gotten away from me:
Love and loss, what plutonium!
What oblivion I could send you to.

They are changing our names in the sky,
making their own insidious designs.
I am one man with just the normal equipment,
saying No, offering little essays to the wind.
They are removing the vowels now.
They are erasing the beginning and the end.

As It Moves

Last week I saw a child
riding an escalator, terrified
when the steps disappeared
and I thought once again
about primitives and the next moment,

the chasm that exists at the tip
of our knowledge. I wanted
to tell the child a story
about the steps, how they
sometimes crawl on their bellies

in order to survive,
how at some safe perfect moment
they rise and become what they are.
But I moved on of course,
went home thinking, oddly,

about a different kind of innocence:
the friend I'd lost to a yoga ashram,
my cousins at the brick plant
and their wives with rosaries.
It was Saturday,

I piled the garbage in the car
and took off
for the dump where seagulls perch
amid orange rinds and broken chairs.
The dump people were out

sifting among the shards.
I can't quite explain it, but
I felt tainted in a proper way
with the world. The seagulls rose.
I wished I could tell my friend:

Look, nothing's simple.
It was almost dusk. I was thinking
the seagull is a comic, filthy bird
magnificent as it moves
upward in imperfect air.

from

NOT DANCING

(1984)

Corners

I've sought out corner bars, lived in corner houses;
　　like everyone else I've reserved
corner tables, thinking they'd be sufficient.
　　I've met at corners
perceived as crossroads, loved to find love
　　leaning against a lamp post
but have known the abruptness of corners too,
　　the pivot, the silence.
I've sat in corners at parties hoping for someone
　　who knew the virtue
of both distance and close quarters, someone with a
　　corner person's taste
for intimacy, hard won, rising out of shyness
　　and desire.
And I've turned corners there was no going back to,
　　corners
in the middle of a room that led
　　to Spain or solitude.
And always the thin line between corner
　　and cornered,
the good corners of bodies and those severe bodies
　　that permit no repose,
the places we retreat to, the places we can't bear
　　to be found.

Atlantic City

To stare at the ocean in winter
　　is to know
　　　　the variety in repetition.

It's to understand repetition's secret
　　link with solace.
　　　　How often I went to it, lonely,

wanting its sexual music, its applause.
　　How often it took my mood
　　　　and deepened it, instructed me

loneliness is nothing special,
　　that I was anybody, a man.
　　　　Yesterday at the blackjack table,

a few hundred yards from the shore,
　　I doubled-down with eleven
　　　　and drew a three. That was it.

I walked up North Carolina to Arctic
　　all alone. The wind suggested
　　　　wonderful movement at sea.

I didn't care. I didn't care if
　　the waves were high and white
　　　　or if the seagulls

were dropping clam shells from the sky.
　　I had a loser's thought: how wise I was
　　　　for not paying to park.

That's what I said to myself
　　far away from myself
　　　　with the ocean now two blocks away;

how wise I was. The houses started to speak
    of ruin. Boards on some windows.
        Wine bottles in doorways.

To stare at a city half in ruin,
    half in glitter,
        is to know why the beach

and its beautiful desolation in winter
    is a fearsome place
        if one comes to it hopeful.

Please, Mister, a man said. In my car,
    hidden under the seat,
        a quarter for the toll booth.

Response to a Letter from France

"We're living in a Socialist paradise.
My mind boggles when I think where you live."

All the trees are in bloom
though the gypsy moths, with their plague
mentality, are blossoming too.
Don't feel sorry for us. We've even learned
to live amid Republicans; the avarice
of gypsy moths is only a little more
mindless, effective. It's okay here.
The ocean isn't perfectly clean
but on good days when I get low enough
the waves push me out ahead of them;
lacking wings or an engine
it's the closest thing to flight.
In France, where life and theory
touch now and then,
I don't doubt your pleasures. But here
there's room enough for incorrect
behavior, which some of us plan on.
There are casinos and fifty or sixty miles
of pines to get lost in.
Socialism makes good sense, sure.
But we actually have four people
who love us, the tennis courts aren't
crowded, our neighbor who has no politics
was generous yesterday for other reasons.
At another time I would offer you
what falls short of promise, the America
outside of me and my part in it.
But not when you feel sorry for us.
I just killed a Brown Recluse spider.
The sun is out. I want you to know
the afternoon is ablaze with ordinary people,
smiling, full of hidden unfulfillment,
everywhere, my friend, everywhere.

South Jersey, July 15, 1981

The Landscape

for Lois

Flood waters in Brigantine.
  And the ocean: a shark
    for every pearl.

So we did the safe thing,
  a house eight miles in
    on the edge of the Barrens,

no pure sand, but the soil
  that has sand in it
    in which scrub oaks grow.

We should have known nothing's safe.
  That love is an ocean too.
    That locks break if touched

just right. And so we live now
  with the doors open, the heart
    learning about the fullness and ache

that comes from letting in.
  The flowers are rose and violet.
    They grow in spite

of where we live. Three miles away
  the old vegetable man thinks
    now of drought, now of rain.

We try to buy from him.
  We try to do the right thing
    but sometimes we lick the palm

of a middleman, change the balance,
  follow our hungers.
    Everyone suffers.

This landscape won't stop.
   This landscape is everywhere.
      Come fall we find ourselves

on our knees, doing what must be done
   in the yard. The cold comes.
      The cold is wisdom

saying huddle together, go inside.
   And the cold follows us
      as far as it can.

In the 20th Century

Someone left green plastic bags full of leaves
   amid fallen leaves at the edge
      of the forest

and there they remained all fall
   like bad modern art,
      like a statement

half thought out, or fully thought out
   by someone half capable
      of thought.

I'd pass them on the road to work
   and would continue on
      in the vague way

most of us continue on, thinking of the
   previous night's quarrel or how
      the sun visor, tilted down,

allowed me to see ahead just enough.
   I was tempted to slit the bags
      open, and once

I dwelt on what this might mean
   to the wilderness, but even then
      I smiled.

It was, I suppose, the smile that accepts
   everything and nothing, the smile
      each of us saves

if not to save ourselves, then to save
   the situation. It's spring now
      near the end

of the century, a natural green mingles
with what looks like
strange bushes, mutants

from some unaccountable marriage—
as if a man, lonely enough
to figure a way,

had gone too far with an experiment.

The Dinner

At dinner, because our hosts had been
    quarreling and couldn't hide it,
        we felt the old need

to charm, to literally enchant
    which also means subdue,
        and they allowed us

to charm them with stories from our day
    which had been full
        of small affections

and a separateness—*a bringing from*—
    and so meant closeness.
        They were kind to allow us

to charm them, feeling as they were
    those ember-like resentments,
        subterranean,

that come from unfinished quarrels.
    But finally charm wasn't equal
        to what they were feeling

and words slipped out, *tones,* then
    the terrible polite talk
        of pass this, pass that, thank you.

One year earlier we were them and knew
    what it would be like after
        we left, how evenings

like this end in separate rooms
    or with violent, not quite
        cathartic lovemaking.

We said goodbye as soon as we could,
    leaving them to what must be
        played out, essential as breathing.

In the car we talked about it,
    not without pleasure.
        There was a low fog

and as we drove it parted, and kept
    parting (What else could it do?)
        all the way home.

Almost Everyone

for Milan Kundera

There are borders toward which
everyone is moving, he thought—
a living room perhaps
where two people begin to float

in the air outside their own lives,
their words empty suitcases
punctuated by travel stickers . . .
a border reached after years

of slippage and sleep.
To invent the future, then,
is to reduce the hazards of being
extinguished by it, he thought,

and conjured a black rainbow
arched over a city,
a giant screen below
on which lovers could be seen

making love. But no matter
how hard he tried
he couldn't help but invent the present,
burdened as he was

by his participation in it,
his desperate hopefulness.
Black rainbows, making love under them . . .
how common!

Yet who could live in the present
with its constant cancellations,
its borders that looked like paths?
Almost everyone, he decided.

The Snow Leopard

After seeing the magnificent blue sheep
high in the Himalayas
Matthiessen wondered if he'd seen enough,
if seeing the snow leopard
wouldn't bring "the desolation of success."
Down here, where we live,
there's just this visible world
and the other world inside it,
the rag lady of Bank Street
sitting with her look-alike dog
and somewhere something else
like the dark rosettes hidden beneath
the fur of the snow leopard.
We buy food at the grocery store,
Scotch enough to last
an ordinary week.
We break down in private,
screaming for love.
Always, up there, there's a Matthiessen
trekking through snow to the top
of something, finding peace
with difficulty, then losing it.
He never saw the snow leopard;
he knew it saw him.
Every day the words "too little"
and "too much" visit each other,
get mixed up.
The boy with orange hair
zips his leather jacket as we pass.
A girl on rollerskates
is half Rockette, half American flag.
We're at sea level, and once
from out of the sea came something like us
as now, climbing steps to our apartment,
we rise higher and higher—
then the unsatisfactory,
the successful key in the lock.

Essay on the Personal

Because finally the personal
is all that matters,
we spend years describing stones,
chairs, abandoned farmhouses—
until we're ready. Always
it's a matter of precision,
what it feels like
to kiss someone or to walk
out the door. How good it was
to practice on stones
which were things we could love
without weeping over. How good
someone else abandoned the farmhouse,
bankrupt and desperate.
Now we can bring a fine edge
to our parents. We can hold hurt
up to the sun for examination.
But just when we think we have it,
the personal goes the way of
belief. What seemed so deep
begins to seem naïve, something
that could be trusted
because we hadn't read Plato
or held two contradictory ideas
or women in the same day.
Love, then, becomes an old movie.
Loss seems so common
it belongs to the air,
to breath itself, anyone's.
We're left with style, a particular
way of standing and saying,
the idiosyncratic look
at the frown which means nothing
until we say it does. Years later,
long after we believed it peculiar

to ourselves, we return to love.
We return to everything
strange, inchoate, like living
with someone, like living alone,
settling for the partial, the almost
satisfactory sense of it.

The Room and the World

The room was room enough for one
or maybe two if the two had just
discovered each other and were one.
Outside of the room was the world
which had a key to the room, and knowing
a little about the world he knew
how pointless it was to change the lock.
He knew the world could enter the room
anytime it wanted, but for the present
the world was content to do its damage
elsewhere, which the television recorded.
Always, he kept in his mind the story of the man
hanging from a cliff, how the wildflowers
growing there looked lovelier than ever.
That was how he felt about his one chair
and the geometry of the hangers in his closet
and the bed that fit him like a body shirt.
Sometimes the world would breathe heavily
outside the door because it was obscene
and could not help itself. It was this
that led him eventually to love the world
for its pressure and essential sadness.
One day he just found himself opening
the door, allowing the inevitable.
The world came in and filled the room.
It seemed so familiar with everything.

The Routine Things
Around the House

When Mother died
I thought: now I'll have a death poem.
That was unforgivable

yet I've since forgiven myself
as sons are able to do
who've been loved by their mothers.

I stared into the coffin
knowing how long she'd live,
how many lifetimes there are

in the sweet revisions of memory.
It's hard to know exactly
how we ease ourselves back from sadness,

but I remembered when I was twelve,
1951, before the world
unbuttoned its blouse.

I had asked my mother (I was trembling)
if I could see her breasts
and she took me into her room

without embarrassment or coyness
and I stared at them,
afraid to ask for more.

Now, years later, someone tells me
Cancers who've never had mother love
are doomed and I, a Cancer,

feel blessed again. What luck
to have had a mother
who showed me her breasts

when girls my age were developing
their separate countries,
what luck

she didn't doom me
with too much or too little.
Had I asked to touch,

perhaps to suck them,
what would she have done?
Mother, dead woman

who I think permits me
to love women easily,
this poem

is dedicated to where
we stopped, to the incompleteness
that was sufficient

and to how you buttoned up,
began doing the routine things
around the house.

Legacy

for my father, Charles Dunn (1905–1967)

1. THE PHOTOGRAPH

My father is in Captain Starns,
a restaurant in Atlantic City.
It's 1950,
I'm there too, eleven years old.
He sold more Frigidaires

than anyone. That's why we're there,
everything free.
It's before the house started
to whisper, before testimony
was called for and lives got ruined.

My father is smiling. I'm smiling.
There's a bowl of shrimp
in front of us.
We have identical shirts on,
short sleeve with little sailboats.
It's before a difference set in

between corniness and happiness.
Soon I'll get up
and my brother will sit next to him.
Mother will click the shutter.
We believe in fairness,

we still believe America
is a prayer, an anthem.
Though his hair is receding
my father's face says nothing
can stop him.

2. THE SECRET

When mother asked him
where the savings went, he said

"the track" and became lost
in his own house, the wastrel,
my mother and her mother
doling out money to him
the rest of his life.

I was sixteen when he told me
the truth, making me his private son,
making anger the emotion
I still have to think about.
I see now that chivalric code
held like a child's song

in the sanctum of his decency,
the error that led to error,
the eventual blur of it all.
And so many nights in the livingroom
the pages of a newspaper being turned

and his sound—Scotch over ice
in a large glass—how conspicuous
he must have felt,
his best gesture gone wrong,
history changed, the days going on and on.

3. THE FAMILY

The family I was part of
was always extended, grandfather
and grandmother on my mother's side
living with us, and grandfather
with a mistress only my father

knew about, beautiful supposedly
and poor. When she began to die
and wouldn't die fast,

when money became love's test,
grandfather had no one

to turn to except my father
who gave him everything.
It was a pact between men,
a handshake and a secret,
then the country turned

to war and all other debts
must have seemed just personal.
Every night the two of them
huddled by the radio waiting for news
of the clear, identifiable enemy.

4. THE SILENCE

My father became a salesman
heavy with silence.
When he spoke he was charming,
allowed everyone to enjoy
not knowing him.

Nights he'd come home drunk
mother would cook his food
and there'd be silence.
Thus, for years, I thought
all arguments were silent
and this is why silence
is what I arm myself with
and silence is what I hate.

Sleep for him was broken speech,
exclamations, the day come back.
Sleep was the surprise

he'd wake up from, on the couch,
still in his clothes.

I carry silence with me
the way others carry snapshots
of loved ones. I offer it
and wait for a response.

5. THE VISITATION

At the airport, on my way to Spain,
he shook my hand too hard,
said goodbye too long.

I spent his funeral in a room
in Cádiz, too poor to fly back
and paying for what I couldn't afford.

The night he died, the night before
the telegram arrived,
something thumped all night

on the flat roof.
It was my father, I think,
come to be let in.

I was in another country,
living on savings. It must have seemed
like heaven to him.

Briefcases

Fifteen years ago I found my father's
   in the family attic, so used
      the shoemaker had to
repair it, and I kept it like love

until it couldn't be kept anymore.
   Then my father-in-law died
      and I got his, almost
identical, just the wrong initials

embossed in gold. It's forty years old,
   falling apart, soon
      there'll be nothing
that smells of father-love and that difficulty

of living with fathers, but I'd prefer
   a paper bag to those
      new briefcases
made for men living fast-forward

or those attaché cases that match
   your raincoat and spring open
      like a salute
and a click of heels. I'm going

to put an ad in the paper, "Wanted:
   Old briefcase, accordion style,"
      and I won't care
whose father it belonged to

if it's brown and the divider keeps
   things on their proper side.
      Like an adoption
it's sure to feel natural before long—

a son without a father, but with this
  one briefcase carrying
    a replica
comfortably into the future,

something for an empty hand, sentimental
  the way keeping is
    sentimental, for *keep-*
sake, with clarity and without tears.

Eggs

I never used to like eggs, that conspicuous
   breaking and ooze like a cow
being slaughtered in the kitchen
   before the steak is served.

And my father wanting his sunny-side-up
   which seemed wrong,
like exposing yourself. But I loved to look
   at unbroken eggs, I loved

to hold them in my hand and toss them up,
   always feeling I knew
how high was too high, always
   coming away clean.

Years later, I'd discover, through Blake,
   you can't get away clean.
You have to know what's more than enough
   to know what's enough,

the game I played was a coward's game.
   I liked my eggs hard boiled
at first, then deviled, ice cold.
   Scrambled was years off;

breaking and cooking them myself—more years.
   One Halloween I stole eggs
from the egg farm, extra large, to throw at girls.
   Loving the shape of eggs,

confused by the shape of girls, I loved
   to see the egg break
on their jeans, loved the screams and the stain.
   Now I suck eggs

after making a little hole in the tip.
   I've made peace with the yolk.
I no longer think of the whites as coming
   face to face with the blind.

I almost can forget how the conglomerates
   have made chickens slaves,
the small cages and the perpetual light.
   I love eggs now,

I love women; I keep my eggs to myself.
   As for the chicken and the egg
I say the egg was first. The egg is perfect.
   It always was.

The chicken, like most children, an afterthought.

An American Film

A rainbow appeared with its promises,
its lore. At a moment like this, I thought,
something might begin for someone else.

The grass was wet. The air chlorophyll.
I walked across the grass
as if I were watching myself

walk across the grass. There was no romance
to the way she waited at the curb
next to the Mazda. She, in fact, was impatient

and I apologized for the lateness
of the hour, the absence
of something graceful, redemptive.

I said, "Look at the rainbow,"
but felt foolish
as if I had said something in song.

Elsewhere things were probably beginning
for other people; kisses, ideas.
We got in the car and drove to Brazil.

No, we got in the car and began
the speaking parts from the life we were in,
then drove to the party.

The sky was a blue helmet
worn by a large invisible clown.
The party was barbecue, backyard.

I knew a good story about a green-head fly
and moved from person to person
telling it. I told it with charm,

hearing myself tell it,
knowing how insignificant it was—
a chance to exhibit pure style.

The woman I arrived with smiled
from across the yard. I felt I should
caress her cheek, take her aside.

Perhaps someone who believed rainbows
were for him was boarding a plane now
ignorant of the story he was in

as only major characters can be.
The hot dogs smelled like good memories.
The bean salad glistened

on its white tray. It was still afternoon,
still only the middle of what
was not much different

from what it felt like, or seemed.

Nova Scotia

Jellyfish washed up
like small blue parachutes
but it was the silent fishing of cranes
that signaled another time
had begun, another world.
I walked to the clam bed
with bucket and pitchfork
and before the sun had fallen
we had steamers
and Black Point darkened
slowly, layer upon layer.
The temperature dropped
into the fifties; how easily we fell
into that smug summer sleep
of people vacationing in the north.

One July, though, out of love
with each other,
we played Frisbee, perfecting
the sidearm, the between-the-legs.
In bed we did it this way,
then that, sad masters of technique.
Then a crane dragged
its damaged leg into the tall reeds,
snapped and hissed
when we got near, would not
let itself be saved.
In the morning
we found its neck ripped—
a weasel's work, pure mischief,
and we felt, no, we were sure
nothing we did or didn't do
could have changed a thing.

Desire

I remember how it used to be
at noon, springtime, the city streets
full of office workers like myself
let loose from the cold
glass buildings on Park and Lex,
the dull swaddling of winter cast off,
almost everyone wanting
everyone else. It was amazing
how most of us contained ourselves,
bringing desire back up
to the office where it existed anyway,
quiet, like a good engine.
I'd linger a bit
with the receptionist,
knock on someone else's open door,
ease myself, by increments,
into the seriousness they paid me for.
Desire was everywhere those years,
so enormous it couldn't be reduced
one person at a time.
I don't remember when it was,
though closer to now than then,
I walked the streets desireless,
my eyes fixed on destination alone.
The beautiful person across from me
on the bus or train
looked like effort, work.
I translated her into pain.
For months I had the clarity
the cynical survive with,
their world so safely small.
Today, walking 57th toward 3rd,
it's all come back,

the interesting, the various,
the conjured life suggested by a glance.
I praise how the body heals itself.
I praise how, finally, it never learns.

Whiteness

On the way to Cottonwood, Minnesota,
along Route 23,
a white horse used to graze—
apparitional, always startling—
like birches suddenly among evergreens.
Eight years have passed
and it's become something clean
and unharnessed for the mind to hold
amid the rush of atrocities;
I see it lifting
its head, cantering toward a barn
where no other animal lived.
There are friends I could ask
but I don't want to know if the horse
is still there or how the winters
might have changed it.
Here there are billboards
on the marshland where egrets
once lived, and that's enough of progress,
enough of the way of things.
Years ago, before experience,
I watched a lovely woman
walk toward me naked,
carrying her shyness like a gift,
and that woman and that horse
are among the photographs untaken
that I plan to die with,
vivid in their whiteness,
pumping blood to and from the heart
even after, maybe for a second or two,
my eyes close and there's nothing.

from

LOCAL TIME

(1986)

Round Trip

1.

I watched the prairie repeat itself
   until it got beautiful, the geometry
     of farms, the flatness

that made interesting the slightest
   undulation. Never had the sky
     touched so far down.

Then, because mood invents landscape,
   the flatness turned irredeemable,
     I felt it go on and on—

something lush and vacant in me
   wished for an edge again,
     a city, an ocean.

I returned east, began to revise
   my childhood, wanted women
     with sharp tongues,

my evening walks shadowy and open
   to possibility. And because the mind
     gets what it wants

but rarely the way it wants it,
   I got mugged on a street corner,
     fear brought home in a real cold sweat

on a real November evening,
   and city life began to insist—
     like jazz, like dream—

it would be nothing but what it was.
   In a rented cabin up north,
     Christmas vacation,

I closed the door and gave whatever in me
    wanted to be alone and pitied
        its hard uncomfortable chair.

But after a while the light
    I didn't believe in
        shone in anyway through the windows,

the walls I had pulled in
    closer and closer
        returned to their proper places.

One day I opened the door
    and it wasn't quite overcast,
        little pieces of sun

reached the tip of my shoe,
    and it was as if I'd touched a breast
        for the first time

and touched it and touched it
    until, having touched it enough,
        I finally saw the blue veins . . .

2.

Ever since, I've been trying to build
    a house of cards amid a house
        of people, hard edges and angles,

each one overlapping. From the beginning
    I've been careful of the one
        that would be too many.

I've kept out of drafts, house-winds.
    The unexpected opening
        of a door, an indelicate voice,

these are the hazards of building
    amid people, amid their enthusiasms
        and secret needs

to destroy. One should be alone
    to build a house of cards.
        One should have a hardwood table,

perfectly flat. One should have none
    of the clutter that comes
        from living a life.

That's why, though, I've been trying
    to build a house of cards
        in a house of people—

to do what's difficult to do
    and so be pleased
        with each card I add,

each moment short of collapse.

3.

There's been a cricket in the livingroom,
    a male because only the male
        is built to sing

or to produce what passes for song.
    It's a mating call, that high sound
        that comes from rubbing

forewing against forewing, plaintive,
    like someone scared blowing
        a little whistle in the dark.

Day and night it's been making that sound
   from somewhere in the room.
      I've opened drawers,

I've pulled chairs away from the wall,
   ready with two paper cups
      to catch it

and take it outside. It came in, I suppose,
   in a confusion of warmth,
      doomed to sing

its song to those who wouldn't understand.
   Now the song grows
      more faint—

why care? it's the end of summer
   and crickets die and come back
      in great, anonymous force.

I'm pulling back the rug, listening
   for what it withholds
      when anyone gets close.

4.

Where does the dark come from?
—The dark comes from the weakness
of the infinity of numbers.
      —Andrea Dunn, age 10

How to leave and come back—the school bus
   instructs my daughter it's easy
      and that for now is good.

She's off again into numbers, words,
    all the necessary confusions.
        History, she believes,

is what happens to others. Biology is what
    she lives with, but hasn't had.
        I'm watching from the window,

the father who knows education
    is all about departures, who knows
        when things are right

nobody comes home the same. The school bus
    has left a hole in the landscape.
        Air fills it now, the low sky

we don't call sky for some reason.
    How to paint a landscape where children
        once played? Swirls and smudges?

My daughter knows where the dark comes from
    and I believe her. She's growing breasts.
        She closes the door to her room.

I'd paint the trees blue because the low sky
    is in them. I'd paint the area white
        where she once did a cartwheel,

maybe with a hint of yellow in it
    for the school bus. Off to the side
        lots of red seemingly out of control

yet orderly, like wildflowers.

5.

Nothing's happening but the wind,
   the ferry rocking its way
      toward Delaware, and Delaware Bay

full of big tankers
   at anchor, seemingly poised.
      It's two hours across,

a talk to give, one night
   away, then two hours back,
      the kind of minor traveling

which tests nothing at home, nothing in self.
   "Travel is the saddest pleasure,"
      a friend once said. He meant

all those hours that exist
   outside of work and play and love.
      The boredom of sailors

must be enormous, as great as the boredom
   of those on land who hope for weather
      to change their lives.

We're bored too, the few of us
   making this trip, off-season, the specter
      of necessity

evident in how we sit and stare.
   Later, I'm thinking, each of us
      will have a story to tell

about the bay and the ships.
   We'll leave out all we can,
      all that is a traveler's life

or a sailor's life. We'll make our friends
    wish they were us, we'll replace experience
        with what we say.

6.

This is one of those stories,
    Minnesota to New Jersey,
        a return home

in search of home, regular departures
    to find the limits
        of home—

impulses finding reasons, words.

The great decisions that change
    a life—hardly decisions
        at all; a wild hunch

or avoidance, the unknown agent x
    coursing through the body
        like a bastard gene.

I'm only sure that collapse
    waits just beyond
        standing still,

the next complacency. Even now,
    my day off, I'm thinking
        I'll get in my car,

get out of here, no rhyme except
    internal rhyme, the clicks
        and bells that go off

when the body has heard itself
and acted. I know where
I'll go—

ball field, casino, deserted beach—
some not-home place
where I can pivot

at supper time, make my way back
as if I'd made a choice.

7.

Last week at this time
Canada geese flapping overhead,
heading south:

impossible to warn them of hunters
up since dawn. A few hours later
three separate phone calls

told me the same person was dead.
By the third my voice
had nothing in it;

it was days before the letting go.
I watched the jays in the yard
chasing smaller birds,

taking all the seed for themselves. That's where
the dark comes from, I thought,
some weakness in the motive

or of the heart, a bunch of jays
exercising their muscle, and *poof,*
nothing's left but jays.

I should have called the dead man's wife.
  I should have reread his poems,
    made him a good ghost

and myself sorrow's perfectly correct man.
  I put on my running shoes,
    ran the full circle

of the park, showered, turned on the
  important game. The whole season
    was on the line,

the announcer said, and it was.
  In a nearby room the noise of others—
    a child's whine, my wife saying No—

mixed with my noise to form
  the familiar. For a while
    nothing tumbled down.

Halves

Once again after dawn before questions
   arrange themselves
into what to do, who to see, and each of us

is most pleasurably alone—the first sounds
   of traffic, muffled
by trees, find their way to the ear;

we don't know what we're hearing, and don't
   care. The light
touches us. We turn toward the dark.

Soon the equally mysterious world of women
   and men, of momentary
common agreement and wild misunderstanding,

will impose itself naturally on the simplest event.
   Anatomy will send
its differing messages to syntax and sense,

and beyond sense—among the senses—
   unbuttoned women
will witness grown men become babies again

and later watch their mouths shape perfectly
   controlled sentences
from distances laughable and immense.

In the morning, though, now, while the secret
   intercoms in our dream rooms
are still open and each separate body knows

but does not reach for what it wants,
   we all live in the same
country, share the same absurd flag.

We keep our eyes closed as long as we can,
    hang on to the vestiges
of night as if we were balancing

two delicate and always vanishing halves.
    Then the alarm, and the body rises
to yearn for what is here and gone.

He/She

Brought up never getting punched
    in the mouth for saying more
        than the situation can bear,

she argues beyond winning,
    screams indictments
        after the final indictment

has skewered him into silence,
    if not agreement.
        The words she uses

mean she is feeling something large
    which needs words, perhaps
        the way Pollack needed paint.

Next day the words are unimportant
    to her, while all
        he's thinking about

are the words she used—
    if recovering from them
        is possible.

Years ago, the schoolyard taught him
    one word too many meant
        broken fingers, missing teeth;

you chose carefully, or you chose war.
    You were the last word
        you let live.

She was in the elsewhere girls were,
    learning other lessons,
        the ones men learn

too late or not at all; you took in,
   cared for, without keeping score
     you shaped a living space

into a kind of seriousness.
   Retract those words, he says.
     But she is only

sensing his reserve, his inability
   to perceive that her wrong words
     meant so much hurt and love.

After the Argument

Whoever spoke first would lose something,
　　that was the stupid
　　　　unspoken rule.

The stillness would be a clamor, a capo
　　on a nerve. He'd stare
　　　　out the window,

she'd put away dishes, anything
　　for some noise. They'd sleep
　　　　in different rooms.

The trick was to speak as if you hadn't
　　spoken, a comment
　　　　so incidental

it wouldn't be counted as speech.
　　Or to touch while passing,
　　　　an accident

of clothing, billowy sleeve against
　　rolled–up cuff. They couldn't
　　　　stand hating

each other for more than one day.
　　Each knew this, each knew
　　　　the other's body

would begin to lean, the voice yearn
　　for the familiar confluence
　　　　of breath and syllable.

When? Who first? It was Yalta, always
　　on some level the future,
　　　　the next time.

This time

there was a cardinal on the bird feeder;
   one of them was shameless enough
      to say so, the other pleased

to agree. And their sex was a knot
   untying itself, a prolonged
      coming loose.

Insomnia

What should be counted was counted
up to a hundred and back.

And sleep came by, I think,
sensed too much movement and left.

Now there's desire meeting absence,
the multiplication of zero,

the mind, as always, holding out
for a perfect convergence

like a diver entering water
without a splash. There's a part

of me terribly stilled and alert,
a silence that won't shut off.

And there's this need to put on the light,
to not sleep on sleep's terms, sleep

which is after all like you, love,
elsewhere and difficult.

Long Term

On this they were in agreement:
everything that can happen between two people
happens after a while

or has been thought about so hard
there's almost no difference
between desire and deed.

Each day they stayed together, therefore,
was a day of forgiveness, tacit,
no reason to say the words.

It was easy to forgive, so much harder
to be forgiven. The forgiven had to agree
to eat dust in the house of the noble

and both knew this couldn't go on for long.
The forgiven would need to rise;
the forgiver need to remember the cruelty

in being correct.
Which is why, except in crises,
they spoke about the garden,

what happened at work,
the little ailments and aches
their familiar bodies separately felt.

Letter Home

for L.

Last night during a thunderstorm,
awakened and half-awake,
I wanted to climb into bed
on my mother's side, be told
everything's all right—
the mother-lie which gives us power
to make it true.
Then I realized she was dead,
that you're the one I sleep with
and rely on, and I wanted you.
The thunder brought what thunder brings.
I lay there, trembling,
thinking what perfect sense we make
of each other when we're afraid
or half-asleep or alone.

Later the sky was all stars,
the obvious ones and those
you need to look at a little sideways
until they offer themselves.
I wanted to see them all—
wanted too much, you'd say—
like this desire to float
between the egg and the grave,
unaccountable, neither lost nor found,
then wanting the comfortable
orthodoxies of home.

I grew up thinking home was a place
you left with a bat
in your hands; you came back dirty
or something was wrong.
Only bad girls were allowed
to roam as often or as far.
Shall we admit

that because of our bodies
your story can never be mine,
mine never yours?
That where and when they intersect
is the greatest intimacy we'll ever have?

Every minute or so a mockingbird
delivers its repertoire.
Here's my blood
in the gray remains of a mosquito.
I know I'm just another slug
in the yard, but that's not what
my body knows.
The boy must die is the lesson
hardest learned.
I'll be home soon. Will you understand
if not forgive
that I expect to be loved
beyond deserving, as always?

Saratoga, 1984

All That We Have

for John Jay Osborn, Jr.

It's on ordinary days, isn't it,
   when they happen,
those silent slippages,

a man mowing the lawn, a woman
   reading a magazine,
each thinking it can't go on like this,

then the raking, the turning
   of a page.
The art of letting pass

what must not be spoken, the art
   of tirade, explosion,
are the marital arts, and we

their poor practitioners, are never
   more than apprentices.
At night in bed the day visits us,

happily or otherwise. In the morning
   the words good morning
have a history of tones; pray to say them

evenly. It's so easy, those moments
   when affection is what
the hand and voice naturally coordinate.

But it's that little invisible cloud
   in the livingroom,
floating like boredom, it's the odor

of disappointment mixing with
   kitchen smells,
which ask of us all that we have.

The man coming in now
  to the woman.
The woman going out to the man.

Parable of the Fictionist

He wanted to own his own past,
be able to manage it
more than it managed him.
He wanted all the unfair
advantages of the charmed.
He selected his childhood,
told only those stories
that mixed loneliness with
rebellion, a boy's locked heart
with the wildness
allowed inside a playing field.
And after he invented himself
and those he wished to know him
knew him as he wished to be known,
he turned toward the world
with the world that was within him
and shapes resulted, versions,
enlargements.
In his leisure he invented women,
then spoke to them about
his inventions, the wish just
slightly ahead of the truth,
making it possible.
All around him he heard
the unforgivable stories
of the sincere, the boring,
and knew his way was righteous,
though in the evenings, alone
with the world he'd created,
he sometimes longed
for what he'd dare not alter,
or couldn't, something immutable
or so lovely he might be changed
by it, nameless but with a name
he feared waits until you're worthy,
then chooses you.

At the Smithville
Methodist Church

It was supposed to be Arts & Crafts for a week,
but when she came home
with the "Jesus Saves" button, we knew what art
was up, what ancient craft.

She liked her little friends. She liked the songs
they sang when they weren't
twisting and folding paper into dolls.
What could be so bad?

Jesus had been a good man, and putting faith
in good men was what
we had to do to stay this side of cynicism,
that other sadness.

O.K., we said. One week. But when she came home
singing "Jesus loves me,
the Bible tells me so," it was time to talk.
Could we say Jesus

doesn't love you? Could I tell her the Bible
is a great book certain people use
to make you feel bad? We sent her back
without a word.

It had been so long since we believed, so long
since we needed Jesus
as our nemesis and friend, that we thought he was
sufficiently dead,

that our children would think of him like Lincoln
or Thomas Jefferson.
Soon it became clear to us: you can't teach disbelief
to a child,

only wonderful stories, and we hadn't a story
nearly as good.

On parents' night there were the Arts & Crafts
all spread out

like appetizers. Then we took our seats
in the church
and the children sang a song about the Ark,
and Hallelujah

and one in which they had to jump up and down
for Jesus.
I can't remember ever feeling so uncertain
about what's comic, what's serious.

Evolution is magical but devoid of heroes.
You can't say to your child
"Evolution loves you." The story stinks
of extinction and nothing

exciting happens for centuries. I didn't have
a wonderful story for my child
and she was beaming. All the way home in the car
she sang the songs,

occasionally standing up for Jesus.
There was nothing to do
but drive, ride it out, sing along
in silence.

The Substitute

When the substitute asked my eighth-grade daughter
　　to read out loud,
she read in Cockney, an accent she'd mastered

listening to rock music. Her classmates laughed
　　of course, and she kept on,
straightfaced, until the merciful bell.

Thus began the week my daughter learned
　　it takes more than style
to be successfully disobedient.

Next day her regular teacher didn't return;
　　she had to do it again.
She was from Liverpool, her parents worked

in a mill, had sent her to America to live
　　with relatives.
At night she read about England, looked at her map

to place and remember exactly where she lived.
　　Soon her classmates
became used to it—just a titter from Robert

who'd laugh at anything. Friday morning,
　　exhausted from learning
the manners and industry of modern England,

she had a stomachache, her ears hurt, there were
　　pains, she said,
all over. We pointed her toward the door.

She left bent over like a charwoman, but near
　　the end of the driveway
we saw her right herself, become the girl

who had to be another girl, a substitute
   of sorts,
in it now for the duration.

The Return

It's taken years to stop the voices
   of the dead
from rising up. Subdued now,

they're content to be on call.
   My father
and Melville and Dostoyevsky—

always complicating the afternoon.
   My mother insisting
with Carlyle on an Everlasting Yea

and I needing to debunk, destroy.
   They've let me go,
and so the true embrace begins.

How to say Father and be small
   and mean it again.

Toward the Verrazano

Up from South Jersey and the low persistent
pines, pollution curls into the sky
like dark cast-off ribbons
and the part of us that's pure camera,
that loves funnel clouds and blood
on a white dress, is satisfied.
At mile 127, no trace of a tree now,
nothing but concrete and high tension
wires, we hook toward the Outerbridge
past Arthur Kill Road where garbage trucks
work the largest landfill in the world.
The windscreens are littered, gorgeous
with rotogravure sections, torn love
letters, mauve once-used tissues. The gulls
dip down like addicts, rise like angels.
Soon we're in traffic, row houses, a college
we've never heard of stark as an asylum.
In the distance there it is, the crown
of this back way in, immense, silvery,
and in no time we're suspended
out over the Narrows by a logic linked
to faith, so accustomed to the miraculous
we hardly speak, and when we do
it's with those words found on picture postcards
from polite friends with nothing to say.

Under the Black Oaks

Because the mind will defend anything
it has found the body doing,
I tell my family I'm out here
because the house is cold,
because it's Saturday,
because I feel like it.
The rock-hard acorns are falling
and I've placed my chair
where one has just fallen,
the beginnings of a theory . . .
The family points out
there are places I could sit
where nothing but the sun
could hit me,
but of course I know about them.
It's one of those mornings
when there seems so much time to fill,
so many correct ways to fill it,
the tedium of virtuous leisure.
The white sky above the oaks
displays its familiar open mockery.
When the wind comes up
the acorns fall like hailstones.
I sit in my chair
listening to how they brush leaves
on the way down, a natural jazz,
thud and silence, then another thud.
My family shouts "Come in, come in,"
but I'm out under the black oaks
and will not budge.

Local Time

The trees were oaks and pines.
The unaffordable house

a little bargain with my soul,
a commitment to the dream

my father lost somewhere
between gin and the dotted line.

The siding was cedar.
The weathervane gun-metal gray.

It was odd how dinner hour
was always approaching,

odd how we counted,
what we counted on.

You folded the napkins
in triangles, set the prehistoric

knives and forks. It all seemed
as if it had happened before.

The night came in layers
through the large windows.

When we finished eating
it was wholly there.

The house had double locks
but in the dark a wrong person

would understand: the windows
were made of glass:

the cat wanted out or in,
the cat so easy to impersonate.

We knew that anyone good
would be unafraid of a light

but we turned on the porch light,
left on an inside light

when we went out, advertised
the signs of our presence.

It was what our parents had done
even in a safer time,

it was all their *be carefuls*
awakening inside us

like slow-dissolving pills,
messages in the bloodstream.

Anyone good, we were sure,
would be bold enough

to work in the open,
would give the illusion

he could be tracked down,
identified.

Still, we left the lights on,
parents ourselves now,

deterring with conventional wisdom
the conventional criminal—

no defense against the simple
knock on the door, the man

with a mask so perfect
we'd shake his hand.

Whatever time it was
it was local time, our time.

What was foreign never occurred
until we heard it here,

wasn't that true?
And didn't enough happen here?

The retarded girl nearby
swallowed stones.

Schultz stepped off that ledge,
everyone knew,

because his house wasn't home.
It was exactly seven o'clock

when we got the news—
time for us to hear

and not forget the orbital tick
of the planet, the not-

so-merry-go-round. But for us
there was food every day,

clothing for every season.
The work we did left some time

for the work we loved.
To complain was obscene.

To lament the drift of any day
marked us American, spoiled,

believers in happiness,
the capital I.

The wars in small countries were ours
if the world was ours.

Whether the world was ours
we couldn't decide.

Our neighbor said everything sucked.
It all was humungous, he said,

and I knew what he meant.
Oh on certain days,

when the smoke-screen of weather
or luck permitted,

we loved the world.
Not to love it, risking nothing,

was to fail only at our desks
sulking over commas and typos

or only in the privacies
of bedroom and kitchen

where we lived largely in miniature.
So we loved the world

when we could. No matter,
our house was a hiding place

and the blood dripped in,
deluged and shamed us.

Where would we go?
To work, to the store,

to the next place on the list?—
as if the next place weren't an alarm

set the night before,
as if there always weren't a dream

to give up, something about to happen
to uncomplicated warmth.

I knew after many hurts
how to hold back

what could hurt me,
how to become hollow, absurd.

Passing churches, I remembered
the old repetitions,

the faked novenas,
but what did I feel, really,

after removing disguise after disguise,
then adding others,

could I know what I felt?
At night the shining

steeple across the lake
was a nuisance or a beacon.

Rocky's all-night bar,
just to the south, was oblivion

or a refuge, often both.
Yet the pleasures were near

like ships just offshore, anchored.
I saw them and peopled them,

heard the music and those ahhs
coming through the air, the walls.

I longed to be a visitor
or the visited, and sometimes I was—

wondering, amid touch and entry,
where the music was

and why intimacy carried with it
such distances.

So many times I lifted
the anchor and let it all go—

in my mind
and from this familiar shore.

I turned further inland
toward bric-a-brac, curios,

the narcosis of purchasing.
I turned toward the skillet,

made something for myself.
But I could sense them,

the replacements coming in—
masted, shapely, moving

through old waters calling to me.
You sensed them, too.

One day, finally daring to speak
of soul, wanting to rescue it

from the unnamed
for my own sake, I decided

it wasn't character
but a candle in the room

of character, visible
around the eyes, the mouth.

It was exciting to discover
I was most aware of it

when it was missing, when nothing lived
or burned behind the eyes

and the voice, a tin box,
couldn't support its words.

Only people wrong for us, I decided,
confused soul

with intelligence or with sorrow.
Discussions with them never touched

down, clicked in. In our true friends
there it was, simply.

It became part of what we meant
when we said their names.

It wasn't enough, of course.
Even in the garden I once

believed spectacular, the tulips
were anybody's pretty girl.

The hyacinths offered such small cheer
I turned to the vegetables

as once I turned to foreign films
for the real.

What could I say?
The garden bloomed

but did not transport?
That I wanted my beauty

a little awkward and odd?
Only the moon flower,

among flowers,
pleased me these days,

lilylike,
opening in the dark.

Every hour the clock struck *now*.
It didn't remind us we would die.

The trees needed to be pruned.
You'd prune the trees.

There was no more milk.
I'd get in the car.

Years ago, when the angels
our parents insisted on

could no longer fly
and our bodies took them in,

it seemed we'd solved by cancellation
how to live on our own.

We bought the house,
the house in the cyclic fog

that looked so new.
It's hours now

since a thunderstorm came,
our little world

of tumult and aftermath
seemingly ratified from above.

Though the sky turned perfect
our dog trembled, hid.

Something was out there,
he was sure. The sparrows,

no less foolish or wise,
returned to the yard and sang.

from

BETWEEN
ANGELS
(1989)

The Guardian Angel

Afloat between lives and stale truths,
    he realizes
he's never truly protected one soul,

they all die anyway, and what good
    is solace,
solace is cheap. The signs are clear:

the drooping wings, the shameless thinking
    about utility
and self. It's time to stop.

The guardian angel lives for a month
    with other angels,
sings the angelic songs, is reminded

that he doesn't have a human choice.
    The angel of love
lies down with him, and loving

restores to him his pure heart.
    Yet how hard it is
to descend into sadness once more.

When the poor are evicted, he stands
    between them
and the bank, but the bank sees nothing

in its way. When the meek are overpowered
    he's there, the thin air
through which they fall. Without effect

he keeps getting in the way of insults.
    He keeps wrapping
his wings around those in the cold.

Even his lamentations are unheard,
    though now,
in for the long haul, trying to live

beyond despair, he believes, he needs
    to believe
everything he does takes root, hums

beneath the surfaces of the world.

Beyond Hammonton

> Night is longing, longing, longing,
> beyond all endurance.
> > —*Henry Miller*

The back roads I've traveled late
at night, alone, a little drunk,
wishing I were someone
on whom nothing is lost,

are the roads by day I take
to the car wash in Hammonton
or to Blue Anchor's
lawnmower repair shop
when the self-propel mechanism goes.

Fascinating how the lamplight
that's beckoned
from solitary windows
gives way to white shutters
and occasionally a woman
in her yard, bending over
something conspicuously in bloom.

So much then is duty, duty, duty,
and so much
with the sun visor tilted
and destination known
can be endured.

But at night . . . no, even at night
so much can be endured.

I've known only one man
who left the road,
followed an intriguing light
to its source.
He told me
that he knocked many times
before it became clear to him
he must break down the door.

Privilege

. . . the privilege of ordinary heartbreak
—*Nadezhda Mandelstam*

I have had such privilege
    and have wept
the admittedly small tears

that issue from it, and for years
    have expected
some terrible random tax

for being born or staying alive.
    It has not come,
though recently in the neighborhood

a child's red ball got loose
    from her, with traffic
bearing down. She was not my child,

I was so happy she was not
    my child.
If one could choose, who wouldn't

settle for deceit or betrayal,
    something
that could be argued or forgiven?

And when I think of Osip, his five
    thousand miles
on a prison train, and the package

you sent him returned months later,
    "The addressee is dead,"
well, that's when the mind that hunts

for comparisons should hesitate,
    then seek
its proper silence. History pressed in

and down, Nadezhda, and you kept living
    and found the words.
I intend no comparison when I say

today the odor of lilacs outside
    my window
is half perfume, half something rotten.

That's just how they smell
    and what I'm used to,
one thing and always the disturbing

insistence of another, fat life itself,
    too much
to let in, too much to turn away.

Loveliness

Years ago, when I was rotten with virtue,
  I believed loveliness
was just a face, a flower,

no underside to it, no dark complication.
  Sometime later
I was sure it couldn't be more than this:

a group of us singing "We Shall Overcome,"
  hands joined, 1968,
the double elixir of anger and conviction

making us gravely intimate.
  But I've felt
the loveliness of a fine moment

passing into the moment that follows,
  I've read books
that slowed down a life

long enough for me to enter it, a life
  so dangerous
and short I've started to rage

at all the postponements in mine,
  all the dead
unforgivably correct afternoons . . .

Last year in a room where survivors
  were gathered
I watched one man's obstinate calm

when it was his turn to thank God,
  how he kept what was his
his, the lovely discrepancy

between what the world expected
   and what he gave.
Or perhaps he was just shy, and I made him

into a man I needed just then. Either way
   I was happy
to witness and be part of something

that ever-so-little could rock the heart,
   tip it
toward fullness. Tonight the anchorman

offers up the brutal in an even voice,
   and the camera zooms in
to the strange loveliness of a bruise;

it reminds me of what a child wrote
   about a sad flower:
the yellow thing in the middle was blue.

Emptiness

I've heard yogis talk of a divine
    emptiness,
the body free of its base desires,

some coiled and luminous god
    in all of us
waiting to be discovered . . .

       and always I've pivoted,

followed Blake's road of excess
    to the same source
and know how it feels to achieve

nothing, the nothing that exists
    after accomplishment.
And I've known the emptiness

of nothing to say, no reason to move,
    those mornings I've built
a little cocoon with the bedcovers

and lived in it, almost happily,
    because what fools
the body more than warmth?

      And more than once

I've shared an emptiness with someone
    and learned
how generous I can be—here,

take this, take this . . .

Tenderness

Back then when so much was clear
   and I hadn't learned
young men learn from women

what it feels like to feel just right,
   I was twenty-three,
she thirty-four, two children, a husband

in prison for breaking someone's head.
   Yelled at, slapped
around, all she knew of tenderness

was how much she wanted it, and all
   I knew
were backseats and a night or two

in a sleeping bag in the furtive dark.
   We worked
in the same office, banter and loneliness

leading to the shared secret
   that to help
National Biscuit sell biscuits

was wildly comic, which led to my body
   existing with hers
like rain that's found its way underground

to water it naturally joins.
   I can't remember
ever saying the exact word, tenderness,

though she did. It's a word I see now
   you must be older to use,
you must have experienced the absence of it

often enough to know what silk and deep balm
    it is
when at last it comes. I think it was terror

at first that drove me to touch her
    so softly,
then selfishness, the clear benefit

of doing something that would come back
    to me twofold,
and finally, sometime later, it became

reflexive and motiveless in the high
    ignorance of love.
Oh abstractions are just abstract

until they have an ache in them. I met
    a woman never touched
gently, and when it ended between us

I had new hands and new sorrow,
    everything it meant
to be a man changed, unheroic, floating.

Sweetness

Just when it has seemed I couldn't bear
   one more friend
waking with a tumor, one more maniac

with a perfect reason, often a sweetness
   has come
and changed nothing in the world

except the way I stumbled through it,
   for a while lost
in the ignorance of loving

someone or something, the world shrunk
   to mouth-size,
hand-size, and never seeming small.

I acknowledge there is no sweetness
   that doesn't leave a stain,
no sweetness that's ever sufficiently sweet . . .

Tonight a friend called to say his lover
   was killed in a car
he was driving. His voice was low

and guttural, he repeated what he needed
   to repeat, and I repeated
the one or two words we have for such grief

until we were speaking only in tones.
   Often a sweetness comes
as if on loan, stays just long enough

to make sense of what it means to be alive,
   then returns to its dark
source. As for me, I don't care

where it's been, or what bitter road
   it's traveled
to come so far, to taste so good.

Kindness

In Manhattan, I learned a public kindness
 was a triumph
over the push of money, the constrictions

of fear. If it occurred it came
 from some deep
primal memory, almost entirely lost—

Here, let me help you, then you me,
 otherwise we'll die.
Which is why I love the weather

in Minnesota, every winter kindness
 linked
to obvious self-interest,

thus so many kindnesses
 when you need them;
praise blizzards, praise the cold.

Kindness of any kind shames me,
 makes me remember
what I haven't done or been.

I met a woman this summer in Aspen
 so kind
I kept testing her to see

where it would end. I thought: how easy
 to be kind in Aspen,
no poverty or crime, each day

a cruise in the blond, expensive streets.
 But I was proof
it wasn't easy, there was an end

to her kindness and I found it;
   I kept wanting
what she didn't have

until she gave me what I deserved.
   If the hearts of men
are merciless, as James Wright said,

then any kindness is water turned
   to wine, it's manna
in the new and populous desert.

The stranger in me knows
   what strangers need.
It might be better to turn us away.

Loneliness

So many different kinds,
yet only one vague word.
And the Eskimos
with twenty-six words for snow,

such a fine alertness
to what variously presses down.
Yesterday I saw lovers
hugging in the street,

making everyone around them
feel lonely, and the lovers themselves—
wasn't a deferred loneliness
waiting for them?

There must be words

for what our aged mothers, removed
in those unchosen homes, keep inside,
and a separate word for us
who've sent them there, a word

for the secret loneliness of salesmen,
for how I feel touching you
when I'm out of touch.
The contorted, pocked, terribly ugly man

shopping in the 24-hour supermarket
at 3 A.M.—a word for him—
and something, please,
for this nameless ache here

in this nameless spot.
If we paid half as much attention

to our lives as Eskimos to snow . . .
Still, the little lies,

the never enough.
No doubt there must be Eskimos
in their white sanctums, thinking
just let it fall, accumulate.

Cleanliness

My cat in a patch of sun
   on the floor, my cat
to whom everything is natural,

puts a little spit on her paws
   and touches herself clean.
Pussy: an epithet, insulting.

Or redeemed, a lover's word
   when only the vulgar
is equal to our wild good humor.

My pussycat in a patch of sun
   licking away
all that's accumulated . . .

Cleanliness; if only we believed,
   without guilt,
in the tongue's intelligence

and the wisdom of genitals,
   wouldn't that erase
a few dirty words? He sucks,

for example. She sucks. How lovely
   as words of praise.
Now my cat, spit-clean,

in a crouch, tail going,
   she's seen
something she wants

and what lover of cats
   wouldn't admire
how perfectly she's made for this?

Happiness

A state you must dare not enter
    with hopes of staying,
quicksand in the marshes, and all

the roads leading to a castle
    that doesn't exist.
But there it is, as promised,

with its perfect bridge above
    the crocodiles,
and its doors forever open.

Between Angels

Between angels, on this earth
absurdly between angels, I
try to navigate

in the bluesy middle ground
of desire and withdrawal,
in the industrial air,
among the bittersweet

efforts of people to connect,
make sense, endure.
The angels out there,
what are they?

Old helpers, half-believed,
or dazzling better selves,
imagined,

that I turn away from
as if I preferred
all the ordinary, dispiriting
tasks at hand?

I shop in the cold
neon aisles
thinking of pleasure,
I kiss my paycheck

a mournful kiss goodbye
thinking of pleasure,
in the evening replenish

my drink, make a choice
to read or love or watch,

and increasingly I watch.
I do not mind living

like this. I cannot bear
living like this.
Oh, everything's true
at different times

in the capacious day,
just as I don't forget
and always forget

half the people in the world
are dispossessed.
Here chestnut oaks
and tenements

make their unequal claims.
Someone thinks of betrayal.
A child spills her milk;
I'm on my knees cleaning it up—

sponge, squeeze, I change nothing,
just move it around.
The inconsequential floor
is beginning to shine.

Each from Different Heights

That time I thought I was in love
and calmly said so
was not much different from the time
I was truly in love
and slept poorly and spoke out loud
to the wall
and discovered the hidden genius
of my hands.
And the times I felt less in love,
less than someone,
were, to be honest, not so different
either.
Each was ridiculous in its own way
and each was tender, yes,
sometimes even the false is tender.
I am astounded
by the various kisses we're capable of.
Each from different heights
diminished, which is simply the law.
And the big bruise
from the longer fall looked perfectly white
in a few years.
That astounded me most of all.

Dancing with God

At first the surprise
of being singled out,
the dance floor crowded
and me not looking my best,
a too-often-worn dress
and the man with me
a budding casualty
of one repetition too much.
God just touched his shoulder
and he left.
Then the confirmation of
an old guess:
God was a wild god,
into the most mindless rock,
but graceful,
looking—this excited me—
like no one I could love,
cruel mouth, eyes evocative
of promises unkept.
I never danced better, freer,
as if dancing were my way
of saying how easily
I could be with him, or apart.
When the music turned slow
God held me close
and I felt for a moment
I'd mistaken him,
that he was Death
and this the famous embrace
before the lights go out.
But God kept holding me
and I him
until the band stopped
and I stood looking at a figure
I wanted to slap

or forgive for something,
I couldn't decide which.
He left then, no thanks,
no sign
that he'd felt anything
more than an earthly moment
with someone who could've been
anyone on earth.
To this day I don't know why
I thought he was God,
though it was clear
there was no going back
to the man who brought me,
nice man
with whom I'd slept
and grown tired,
who danced wrong,
who never again
could do anything right.

The Listener

The town was nameless because it could
   have been any town
one was new to, alone in, and he walked

its main street with a hesitant sense
   of possibility,
a sizing up, all the shops in a row,

this open door or that. He stopped
   to look in a window,
and, seeing no one but himself in the glass,

corrected a few strands of hair.
   In the street
women were everywhere, prolific

because he chose to see them
   singularly.
He was after all a traveler, alert

to the small deprivations that travelers—
   . suspended as they are—
notice and feel. The women in the town

were secretly waiting to be spoken to,
   deeply,
some unaddressed part of them

closed down for too long. And he knew
   the words, interrogative,
concerned, and how to wait for an answer,

showing with his eyes how much he wanted it
   until it came.
Most of them had never known such intimacy,

a man listening, the extraordinary fact
   of a man listening,
which was like a touch to them,

a touch, say, on the forehead
   when they felt
totally exposed. He entered

The Half Moon Café. A man
   with a John Deere hat
sat alone. Two women, lonely, he knew,

because of their public voices,
   were finishing dessert.
It always went like this. He'd ask

something about the town. Then he'd ask
   something else.

The Man Who Closed Shop

To allow himself to be properly held
   he had to let his body
soften, give it unguarded, willingly,

to her. It meant suspension
   of achievement,
a celebration in a country

without government. Always he desired
   the getting there,
loved, in fact, getting lost

on the way. But too often,
   too soon,
he'd think of the office

or a program he was missing
   on TV. He'd feel
his body pull back into itself

like a man closing his own shop
   midday
for reasons he didn't understand.

He'd roll away, thinking to himself
   "This is pleasure, too,"
knowing he'd need different words—

yet whatever his explanation
   she knew it
beforehand, several touches ago.

Mon Semblable

No man has ever dared to describe himself as he truly is.
—*Albert Camus*

I like things my way
every chance I get.
A limit doesn't exist

when it comes to that.
But please, don't confuse
what I say with honesty.

Isn't honesty the open yawn
the unimaginative love
more than truth?

Anonymous among strangers
I look for those
with hidden wings,

and for scars
that those who once had wings
can't hide.

Though I know it's unfair,
I reveal myself
one mask at a time.

Does this appeal to you,
such slow disclosures,
a lifetime perhaps

of almost knowing one another?
I would hope you, too,
would hold something back,

and that you'd always want
whatever unequal share
you had style enough to get.

Altruism is for those
who can't endure their desires.
There's a world

as ambiguous as a moan,
a pleasure moan
our earnest neighbors

might think a crime.
It's where we could live.
I'll say I love you,

which will lead, of course,
to disappointment,
but those words unsaid

poison every next moment.
I will try to disappoint you
better than anyone ever has.

Letting the Puma Go

I'll make a perfect body, said God,
and invent ways to make it fail.
   —lines removed from the poem

He liked to watch the big cats.
He liked their beautiful contempt,
yet imagined how they might change
and love him
and stretch out near his feet
if he were to let them go.
And of course he wanted
to let them go
as he wanted to let himself go,
grateful for the iron bars, the lock.
He'd heard the tiger succeeds
only once in twenty hunts—
the fragile are that attuned
and that fast—
and was confused again about God,
the god who presided here.
He'd watch the tigers at feeding time,
then turn to the black panther,
its languid fierce pacing, and know
it was possible not to care
if the handsome get everything.
Except for the lions.
Hadn't the lions over the years
become their names, like the famous?
But he could spend half an afternoon
with those outfielders,
the pumas, cheetahs, leopards.
So this is excellence, he imagined:
movement toward the barely possible,
the puma's dream
of running down a hummingbird
on a grassy plain.
And then he'd let the puma go;
just before closing time

he'd wish-open its cage
and follow it into the suddenly
uncalm streets,
telling all the children it was his.

His Music

It wasn't that he liked being miserable.
He simply had grown used to wearing
a certain face, become comfortable
with his assortment of shrugs and sighs.
His friends said How are you?—
and prepared their sympathy cards.
Miserable was his style, his insurance
against life's frightening, temporary joys.
And when the truly awful happened,
some rejection or loss,
how ready he was for its aftermath,
how appropriate his posture, his words.
Yet when she said she loved him
something silently wild and molecular
began its revolution; he would've smiled
if the news from the distant provinces
of his body had reached him in time.
He frowned. And did not allow the short sigh
which would have meant pleasure
but now, alone, was just old breath
escaping, the long ahhhh, that music
which soothed him, and was his song.

Competition

Because he played games seriously
 and therefore knew grace
comes hard, rises through the cheap

in us, the petty, the entire history
 of our defeats,
he looked for grace in his opponents,

found a few friends that way
 and so many others
he could never drink with, talk to.

He learned early never to let up,
 never to give
a weaker opponent a gift

because so many times he'd been
 that person
and knew the humiliation in it,

being pandered to, a bone for the sad
 dog.
And because he remembered those times

after a loss when he'd failed
 at grace—
stole from the victor

the pleasures of pure victory
 by speaking
about a small injury or the cold

he wasn't quite over—he loved
 those opponents
who'd shake hands and give credit,

save their true and bitter stories
   for their lovers, later,
when all such lamentations are comic,

the sincere *if onlys* of grown men
   in short pants.
Oh there were people who thought

all of it so childish; what to say
   to them, how to agree,
ever, about dignity and fairness?

To a Terrorist

For the historical ache, the ache passed down
which finds its circumstance and becomes
the present ache, I offer this poem

without hope, knowing there's nothing,
not even revenge, which alleviates
a life like yours. I offer it as one

might offer his father's ashes
to the wind, a gesture
when there's nothing else to do.

Still, I must say to you:
I hate your good reasons.
I hate the hatefulness that makes you fall

in love with death, your own included.
Perhaps you're hating me now,
I who own my own house

and live in a country so muscular,
so smug, it thinks its terror is meant
only to mean well, and to protect.

Christ turned his singular cheek,
one man's holiness another's absurdity.
Like you, the rest of us obey the sting,

the surge. I'm just speaking out loud
to cancel my silence. Consider it an old impulse,
doomed to become mere words.

The first poet probably spoke to thunder
and, for a while, believed
thunder had an ear and a choice.

About the Elk and the Coyotes
That Killed Her Calf

for Richard Selzer

The coyotes know it's just
   a matter of time,
but the elk will not let them

have her calf. You describe
   how they attack
and pull back, and how she goes on

repelling them, occasionally licking
   her calf's face,
until exhausted she turns

and gives it all up. So the elk,
   with her fierce
and futile resistance in which we

recognize something to admire,
   is held up
against the brilliant, wild

cunning of the coyotes.
   I love your sense
that the natural world stinks

and is beautiful and how important it is
   to have favorites.
Some part of us we'd like to believe

is essentially us, sides with the elk.
   Ah but tomorrow,
desperate, and night falling fast

and with a different sense of family . . .

Urgencies

I woke to the sound of rain, and lay there
   canceling
parts of the day. Now I couldn't patch

the leaking roof; something funny
   about that,
one of the temporary pleasures

of the mind. My wife was still asleep.
   I wanted to disturb her,
tell her about the irony of rain

and Saturday mornings and leaks.
   I put on my robe,
went to the window. In the grayness

there were different shades of gray.
   I don't know why
that seemed sad, or why

I suddenly wanted to pull apart
   the curtains,
let some cruelty in. The rain

was steady and this was spring.
   There were things
to be happy for, the flowers for example,

the tree frogs and their alto songs.
   I wanted to tell my wife
about the grass as if she'd never

heard of grass, the crazy speed at which
   it grows in May,
a few things I'd thought of and noticed

since the night has passed. But her sleep
   was persistent,
a deep and now annoying sleep.

I went downstairs. The cat was waiting
   to be fed and had practiced
certain gestures of affection,

which I loved, so I'd open the can.
   It was understood;
if he'd purr and rub his head

against mine, all anxiety would end,
   the morning
become languorous and his.

I put the coffee on and broke the eggs.
   It was the wooden spoon,
the flame and me against the protoplasmic

sprawl; we made the center hold.
   I wanted my wife
down here, I wanted her in some usual

place doing some usual things.
   What I had to say to her
was so insignificant only she would understand.

I sat down to eat. The rain picked up.
   A man could die
just like that. Or begin to slide.

I started to clank the dishes,
   make some noise.

Wanting to Get Closer

Oh vanity
makes everything a little lovelier.
I like those people
who feel a vagueness exists
without them, who see in themselves
a hundred possible improvements.
And the fictions! How the thing
looked at changes as it changes
the looker. Even the physicist
stands here rather than there,
tipping the universe accordingly.

To speak of Narcissus is to speak
of conviction. What matter
that he saw himself
in the glassy water? For once
his aesthetic found its embodiment
and he went to meet it, dying
(I'd like to think) of amazement.
Reader, whom I must not address,
once again I'm standing
in front of a mirror.
I want to get close, then closer.
The image doesn't interest me.

Naturally

When I die there'll be evidence
   such as this
of a life, everything, all of it,

arranged for effect, and only true
   if believed
to be true, and no matter how sad

a few people might feel,
   I know joy
will be holding out

in some muscled corner
   of their hearts,
the sky will simply darken

at the proper time while the light
   will be blinding
elsewhere, in another language.

Walking the Marshland

Brigantine Wildlife Refuge, 1987

It was no place for the faithless,
    so I felt a little odd
walking the marshland with my daughters,

Canada geese all around and the blue
    herons just standing there,
safe, and the abundance of swans.

The girls liked saying the words,
    gosling,
egret, whooping crane, and they liked

when I agreed. The casinos were a few miles
    to the east.
I liked saying craps and croupier

and sometimes I wanted to be lost
    in those bright
windowless ruins. It was early April,

the gnats and black flies
    weren't out yet.
The mosquitoes hadn't risen

from their stagnant pools to trouble
    paradise and to give us
the great right to complain.

I loved these girls. The world
    beyond Brigantine
awaited their beauty and beauty

is what others want to own.
    I'd keep that
to myself. The obvious

was so sufficient just then.
   Sandpiper. Red-wing
blackbird. "Yes," I said.

But already we were near the end.
   Praise refuge,
I thought. Praise whatever you can.

from

LANDSCAPE AT THE
END OF THE
CENTURY
(1991)

Update

to Bartleby

There is the sky and here
is the grass, he said to you,
but you couldn't be fooled.
Not much has changed.
Nearby is the slavish city
and once upon a time
there was a God.
You'd be among our homeless,
nameless and cold.
The elms are dead, and fires
have taken acres of pines.
You'd never be able to tell
that the ocean has changed.
Here is the wind
and there are the balloons
the children have let go.
I know where I am, you said;
office, prison,
all the same to you.
There's the path
up the mountain where often
bear tracks have been seen,
and here the tree on which lovers
carved their names.
First they grew apart,
then they died.
The bears were interested
in berries. Like you,
they kept to themselves.
Love would have changed
everything for you,
but Melville was wise;
you'd have been forgettable,
bringing the costly bacon home.
The imagination still opens the door

we hesitate before,
still turns on the light.
Here is the book
in which you live
and here's what you've spawned:
drop-outs, slackards,
and a kind of dignity, a quaint
contagious way to refuse.
In the face of decency
how did you see the absurd?
The system still shows
its sweetest face, still sends out
an honest man with a smile.
Here are the foul-mouthed
gorgeous gulls,
and these are the walls
in which we live,
in which your heirs
call themselves free.
It's the end of the century;
almost everyone dreams of money
or revenge.

What They Wanted

They wanted me to tell the truth,
so I said I'd lived among them
for years, a spy,
but all that I wanted was love.
They said they couldn't love a spy.
Couldn't I tell them other truths?
I said I was emotionally bankrupt,
would turn any of them in for a kiss.
I told them how a kiss feels
when it's especially undeserved;
I thought they'd understand.
They wanted me to say I was sorry,
so I told them I was sorry.
They didn't like it that I laughed.
They asked what I'd seen them do,
and what I do with what I know.
I told them: find out who you are
before you die.
Tell us, they insisted, what you saw.
I saw the hawk kill a smaller bird.
I said life is one long leave-taking.
They wanted me to speak
like a journalist. I'll try, I said.
I told them I could depict the end
of the world, and my hand wouldn't tremble.
I said nothing's serious except destruction.
They wanted to help me then.
They wanted me to share with them,
that was the word they used, share.
I said it's bad taste
to want to agree with many people.
I told them I've tried to give
as often as I've betrayed.
They wanted to know my superiors,
to whom did I report?

I told them I accounted to no one,
that each of us is his own punishment.
If I love you, one of them cried out,
what would you give up?
There were others before you,
I wanted to say, and you'd be the one
before someone else. Everything, I said.

The Woman on Edgehill Road

Ah, thinks the man, that woman walking
    Edgehill Road, weeping,
has a story to tell, what luck to find
    a woman like this.

All day he's wanted to tell *his* story,
    but he knows the woman
has the weight of tears on her side, the primacy
    of outward grief;

there'd be long listening before it would be
    his sweet time.
He's in his slow car, slow because he wants
    it slow—

last night's shouting and slammed door
    putting him on cruise.
The woman is gesturing now, speaking out loud.
    Once, no doubt,

the person she so hates was a god.
    It's not funny,
but isn't it always funny, thinks the man,
    to someone?

He would like to pull up close. "This is
    the sadness car,"
he might say, "and this the weeping seat
    and this the seat

where you keep things inside." And they
    would take turns
all the way into the next state
    where suddenly

they wouldn't need each other, so bored
    would they be with sadness
and themselves. But the man is burdened
    by the history of men,

by every man who's yelled or whispered
    from a car
on a road like this. He doesn't want
    to scare her

and, besides, he lacks charm when he's sad.
    When he's sad
everything sounds wrong. He accelerates
    into silence,

and will never tell his story as he might have,
    though why should anyone care?
Already it's lost as he turns into Weaver Lane
    toward home,

has become a little more orderly, understood.
    And the woman, too,
he's thinking that years from now
    her ugly trembling lip

will be steady, she'll remember this afternoon
    in the past tense,
all her pauses, everything she omits,
    will be correct.

Smiles

It was as if a pterodactyl had landed,
   cocky
and fabulous amid the earth-bound,

so it's not difficult to understand
   why I smiled
when I saw that Rolls-Royce

moving slowly on the Black Horse Pike
   past the spot
where Crazy Eddie's once was.

Just one week earlier I'd seen a man,
   button-downed and wing-tipped,
reading *Sonnets to Orpheus* in paperback

at the mall's Orange Julius stand.
   My smile was inward,
I craved some small intimacy,

not with him, but with an equal lover
   of the discordant,
another purchaser adrift among the goods.

Sometimes I'd rather be ankle-deep
   in mud puddles,
swatting flies with the Holsteins,

I'd rather be related to that punky boy
   with purple hair
walking toward the antique shop

than talk with someone who doesn't know
   he lives
in *"Le Siècle de Kafka,"* as the French

dubbed it in 1984. The state of New Jersey,
    that same year,
refused to pay Ai for a poetry reading

because her name needed two more letters,
    which produced my crazy smile,
though I wanted to howl too, I wanted to meet

the man who made the rule, kiss him hard
    on his bureaucratic lips,
perhaps cook for him a scalding bowl

of alphabet soup. Instead we added two asterisks
    and the check came!
Four spaces on a form all filled in

and the state was pleased, which is why
    I'm lonely
for the messiness of the erotic, lonely

for that seminal darkness that lurks
    at birthday parties, is hidden
among hugs at weddings, out of which

smiles, even if wry or bitter, are born.
    In the newspaper today
it says that the man who robbed a jewelry store

in Pleasantville, crippling the owner,
    wasn't happy
with his life, was just trying to be happier.

And in Cardiff, just down the road, someone
    will die at the traffic circle
because history says so, history says *soon,*

and that's the circle I must take
   in my crushable Toyota
if I wish to stay on the Black Horse Pike,

and I do.

Ordinary Days

The storm is over; too bad, I say.
   At least storms are clear
about their dangerous intent.

Ordinary days are what I fear,
   the sneaky speed
with which noon arrives, the sun

shining while a government darkens
   a decade, or a man
falls out of love. I fear the solace

of repetition, a withheld slap in the face.
   Someone is singing
in Portugal. Here the mockingbird

is a crow and a grackle, then a cat.
   So many things
happening at once. If I decide

to turn over my desk, go privately wild,
   trash the house,
no one across town will know.

I must insist how disturbing this is—
   the necessity
of going public, of being a fool.

Regardless

Once, my father took me to the Rockaways
    during a hurricane
to see how the ocean was behaving,

which made my mother furious, whose love
    was correct, protective.
We saw a wooden jetty crumble. We saw water

rise to the boardwalk, felt the wildness
    of its spray.
That night: silence at dinner, a storm

born of cooler, more familiar air.
    My father
always rode his delightful errors

into trouble. Mother waited for them, alertly,
    the way the oppressed
wait for their historical moment.

Weekdays, after six, I'd point my bicycle
    toward the Fleet Street Inn
to fetch him for dinner. All his friends

were there, high-spirited lonelies, Irish,
    full of laughter.
It was a shame that he was there, a shame

to urge him home. Who was I then but a boy
    who had learned to love
the wind, the wind that would go its own way,

regardless. I must have thought damage
    is just what happens.

From the Manifesto of the Selfish

Because altruists are the least sexy
   people on earth, unable
to say "I want" without embarrassment,

we need to take from them everything
   they give,
then ask for more,

this is how to excite them, and because
   it's exciting
to see them the least bit excited

once again we'll be doing something
   for ourselves,
who have no problem taking pleasure,

always desirous and so pleased to be
   pleased, we who above all
can be trusted to keep the balance.

Bringing It Down

The man watched
   and though he was accustomed
      to what he saw

it struck him he was looking
   at a sky
      that could hold a jet

and no longer a god.
   And against decency,
      for reasons

he didn't want to know,
   he began to bring
      that jet down,

the plane getting larger
   as it descended
      out of control,

a fire in the fuselage,
   then the few lives
      he'd help save.

The man simply wanted to feel
   at ease, that's all.
      That's how he thought:

first some wildness, then
   a healing ease.
      He wanted one person

he'd brought down
   to be whole,
      smiling up at him,

her seatbelt still on.
He brought on
the dark clouds.

From where he stood
he brought them
from the west

and the noise began.
What harm
in a little more damage?

He brought the wind, the hail.
There weren't enough
rewards in this world,

he felt, for the things
he imagined,
but didn't do.

The man went inside.
He had some
unanswered letters

on his desk. One he'd never
answer because it was
too detailed and thoughtful,

full of a love he couldn't match.
He'd save no lives,
he thought.

Even if he rummaged
through the wreckage, everyone
would be too far gone.

He put the letter in a box
   of letters, the box
      he expected to astound him

when he was old. The lost, the dead
   would speak to him then.
      He'd make sure of that.

The Sudden Light and the Trees

Syracuse, 1969

My neighbor was a biker, a pusher, a dog
    and wife beater.
In bad dreams I killed him

and once, in the consequential light of day,
    I called the Humane Society
about Blue, his dog. They took her away

and I readied myself, a baseball bat
    inside my door.
That night I heard his wife scream

and I couldn't help it, that pathetic
    relief; her again, not me.
It would be years before I'd understand

why victims cling and forgive. I plugged in
    the Sleep-Sound and it crashed
like the ocean all the way to sleep.

One afternoon I found him
    on the stoop,
a pistol in his hand, waiting,

he said, for me. A sparrow had gotten in
    to our common basement.
Could he have permission

to shoot it? The bullets, he explained,
    might go through the floor.
I said I'd catch it, wait, give me

a few minutes and, clear-eyed, brilliantly
    afraid, I trapped it
with a pillow. I remember how it felt

when I got it in my hand, and how it burst
   that hand open
when I took it outside, a strength

that must have come out of hopelessness
   and the sudden light
and the trees. And I remember

the way he slapped the gun against
   his open palm,
kept slapping it, and wouldn't speak.

Turning Fifty

I saw the baby possum stray too far
and the alert red fox claim it
on a dead run while the mother watched,
dumb, and, oddly, still cute.
I saw this from my window
overlooking the lawn surrounded
by trees. It was one more thing
I couldn't do anything about,
though, truly, I didn't feel very much.
Had my wife been with me,
I might have said, "the poor possum,"
or just as easily,
"the amazing fox." In fact
I had no opinion about what I'd seen,
I just felt something dull
like a small door being shut,
a door to someone else's house.

That night, switching stations, I stopped
because a nurse had a beautiful smile
while she spoke about triage and death.
She was trying to tell us
what a day was like in Vietnam.
She talked about holding
a soldier's one remaining hand,
and doctors and nurses hugging
outside the operating room.
And then a story of a nineteen-year-old,
almost dead, whispering "Come closer,
I just want to smell your hair."

When my wife came home late, tired,
I tried to tell her
about the possum and the fox,
and then about the young man

who wanted one last chaste sense
of a woman. But she was interested
in the mother possum,
what did it do, and if I did anything.
Then she wanted a drink, some music.
What could be more normal?
Yet I kept talking about it
as if I had something to say—
the dying boy
wanting the nurse to come closer,
and the nurse's smile as she spoke,
its pretty hint of pain,
the other expressions it concealed.

When the Revolution Came

When the revolution came we were lounging at home.
They were suddenly dancing in Prague
and we were setting the table, forks on the left,
knives on the right. All our categories were old.
We should have been making love when the Wall
came down. We should have been turning a phrase.
When the revolution came it was the widening of a crack,
the lifting of gray. The tyrants just stepped down.
Some apologized. History turned in its enormous grave.
When the revolution came we were wearing
the work boots of the miner, the downy vest
of the longshoreman, thinking of style.
When the revolution came we were counting
our deprivations as only the full-bellied can.
Walesa raised his hands in triumph. Our throats
tightened. East Berliners strolled into the land
of commerce; our throats tightened again.
Were we thinking of ourselves when the revolution
came? And did we feel a little smug?
It was a cold December when the century changed,
colder for some. It was not yet Christmas,
not yet Romania, that harsh gift, blood-soaked,
its past opened up. Every year we promised
to want a little less, and always failed.
When the revolution came we watched the insistence
of crowds, almost free enough to become us.

White Collar

He has to put it somewhere, the violence
   from without. Each day
it comes from newspapers and the streets,

so ordinary now it lives with white lies
   and spoiled milk,
yet it amazes him how easily it mixes

with his own, that there's a place for it,
   located no place
in particular, just part of him

like fat—rapes, tortures, massacres,
   all taken in
and covered by nerve endings half dead.

Oh, once he had feelings equal to what
   he should feel,
in the old neighborhood, years ago . . .

He's a citizen, but now always
   of somewhere else,
the marshland pushing him to the city, the city

to the mountains, the enormous country itself
   inclining him inward
to his room with its shelves of private anthems.

He believes that someone intimate with need
   and scarcity,
crack-driven, knife-happy, nothing to do

until the pawnshop opens, is moving randomly
   in his direction.
It's inevitable, this touch of the personal.

In his violence place, a stirring, as if his body
    and its repressed
outlaw history might be readying itself

for action. But that person never arrives,
    chooses a darker house
with the gate open, no sign of a dog.

Not the Occult

Because I was slow with girls
and didn't understand
they might like to be touched,
my girlfriend took my hand
and placed it on her breast.
We were sixteen. I just
left it there
as if I were memorizing,
which in fact I was.
It was all research and dream,
some fabulous connection
between my hand and her breathing,
then I was breathing like that too.

I've always been drawn
to such ordinary mysteries, women
and men, the broken bridge
between us. I like thinking
about night falling in a house
where anything can happen, and has,
strangers coming in
from their public outposts,
the drift of history
behind any wish to explain.
How to say what can't be said
across a table, or bed?

It's not the occult
and those obvious stakes
in the heart
that make me wonder.
And I confess
I have trouble speaking to people
fond of outer space.
I don't like riddles.

I'm tired of ambiguity's
old academic hush. Still . . .

things happen,
and simply to record them
is often to deceive,
is even sometimes to mimic fog,
the way it's perfectly
yet inadequately clear about itself.

I'm thinking of that woman
returning from the restroom,
unable to recognize her husband.
She wasn't old, he hadn't disappeared,
though she perhaps had lost him.
Where is my husband? she asked the waiter,
who pointed toward the table.

And I'm thinking of the time
we lay ourselves down
among the dwarf pines,
looked up at the sky.
Nothing was new up there,
and down here the words for love
stuck in their history of abuse.
Angel, I wanted to say, meaning darling,
it seems heroic how we survive each other,
heroic that we try.

I'm thinking of the power of loveliness
to sadden.

Oh once there was such awe,
such a pure desire to praise.
There's not one of us
who inspires as much.

But I love the local and crude
somehow made beautiful, all the traces
of how it got that way erased.
And I love the corporeal body itself,
designed to fail,
and the mind, the helpless mind,
so often impelled to think about it.

A Secret Life

Why you need to have one
is not much more mysterious than
why you don't say what you think
at the birth of an ugly baby.
Or, you've just made love
and feel you'd rather have been
in a dark booth where your partner
was nodding, whispering yes, yes,
you're brilliant. The secret life
begins early, is kept alive
by all that's unpopular
in you, all that you know
a Baptist, say, or some other
accountant would object to.
It becomes what you'd most protect
if the government said you can protect
one thing, all else is ours.
When you write late at night
it's like a small fire
in a clearing, it's what
radiates and what can hurt
if you get too close to it.
It's why your silence is a kind of truth.
Even when you speak to your best friend,
the one who'll never betray you,
you always leave out one thing;
a secret life is that important.

Landscape at the End of the Century

The sky in the trees, the trees mixed up
with what's left of heaven, nearby a patch
of daffodils rooted down
where dirt and stones comprise a kind
of night, unmetaphysical, cool as a skeptic's
final sentence. What this scene needs
is a nude absentmindedly sunning herself
on a large rock, thinks the man fed up
with nature, or perhaps a lost tiger,
the maximum amount of wildness a landscape
can bear, but the man knows and fears
his history of tampering with everything,
and besides to anyone who might see him
he's just a figure in a clearing
in a forest in a universe
that is as random as desire itself,
his desire in particular, so much going on
with and without him, moles humping up
the ground near the daffodils, a mockingbird
publishing its cacophonous anthology,
and those little Calvinists, the ants,
making it all the more difficult
for a person in America
to close his office, skip to the beach.
But what this scene needs are wisteria
and persimmons, thinks the woman
sunning herself absentmindedly on the rock,
a few magnificent words that one
might want to eat if one were a lover
of words, the hell with first principles,
the noon sun on my body, tempered
by a breeze that cannot be doubted.
And as she thinks, she who exists
only in the man's mind, a deer grazes

beyond their knowing, a deer tick riding
its back, and in the gifted air
mosquitoes, dragonflies, and tattered
mute angels no one has called upon in years.

Loves

I love the past, which doesn't exist
until I summon it, or make it up,
and I love how you believe
and certify me by your belief,
whoever you are, a fiction too,
held together by what? Personality?
Voice? I love abstractions, I love
to give them a nouny place to live,
a firm seat in the balcony
of ideas, while music plays.
I love them more than hard evidence
and shapely stones, more than money,
which can buy time, but not enough.
I love love, for example,
its diminishments and renewals,
I love being the stupidest happy kid
on the block.
          And what's more interesting
than gossip about love? When I tell
a friend that my life is falling apart,
what a subject for him
to dine out on! What secrets for him
never to tell a soul, except those
souls to whom he tells everything.
I love how a good story insists
on being told.
     When I betrayed, I loved chaos,
loved my crazed version of sane.
When I was betrayed, I loved fidelity,
home. I love more carefully now.
But never to have betrayed, admit it,
is a kind of lethargy or rectitude,
a failure, pure.
     I love the way my cat Peaches
brought the live rat to the door

looking for praise. I love his dignity
when he seeks company, or turns away.
Of all fruits, plums.
Of vegetables, mushrooms sautéed
in garlic and wine.
I love that a list like this
always must extend itself,
and must exclude, slash.
Loving: such a ruthless thing.
      I love shifting from second
to third, that little smooth jerk
into speed, though it's not exactly speed
I want, but being in the middle of speed
as in the somewhere of good sex,
those untimed next things
occurring on time. I love the moment
at the races when they're all in the gate,
such power
not yet loose, and I love the race itself,
how the good jockey tempers and saves,
then dares. I love something to yell for,
something to bet my sweet life on
again and again.
      I love the ocean in winter,
that desolation from which I can return,
solitude that's sought and cradled,
the imaginings one leans toward
at a jetty's end. Often, out there,
I've remembered what I love
about my marriage, turns and gatherings,
odd sacrifices, the sticking it out.
In retrospect, and only in retrospect,
I love a cataclysm that heals.
I love knowing that a marriage
must shed its first skin

in order to survive, must shed again.
Wreckage, thy name is progress.
It hurts just to think of you.
       I love the power
not to use power, the weaker wolf
offering his jugular
and the stronger wolf refusing.
I love how breasts curve and reach
different crests, the long nipple, the
minor crown, the hard unbuttoned button,
each a gift. The faith we put
in a lover's mouth! I love when
a distinction vanishes
between infantile and adult.
     How alert I am to circumstance
when I'm leaving for a while,
or being left. I love the psychology
of kisses at such times, the guilt kiss
and the complaint kiss, the kiss
with a question in it.
And who docsn't love to be the one
who returns, all puckered and alive?
       I love the game-winning shot
that isn't an accident, the shot prepared for
all one's life, practice and talent
metamorphosed into a kind of ease.
I love the trouble
skill can get you out of, and the enlivening
pressures of boundaries and time.
No moment as lovely as the surpassing moment!
Oh poetry, oh the importance of ground
when leaving the ground.
       I love the carpenter bees
in spring, mating in air, and I don't mind
the holes they make in my house

or the innocent buzzing of my head.
Murderer, you're just a sting away.
Murderer, it's you who loves that weasel
in Nova Scotia, the graceful
treacherous one. Amazing
how he got through the chicken wire,
slinky as a mouse.
I love thinking of him returning
to the sanctuary of weasels, calm,
matter-of-fact. And something else in me
loved the blue jay
who all summer dive-bombed my cat,
the only justice it could deliver
for many blue deaths.
          "I want to be consistent
with the truth as it reveals itself
to me," Gandhi said, and I felt
the hard permission right words give us
to disobey, to become ourselves.
I loved thinking that integrity
might be fluid, and still do,
though the indulgent, rudderless
and without shame, love to think so too,
and the truth is
the indulgent are my careless brothers
half the time.
    I love the way sorrow and lust
can be companions. I love the logic
of oxymorons, and how paradox helps us
not to feel insane. Aren't facts
essentially loose, dull? I love
that an accident that doesn't occur
is replaced by one that does.
It's the personal that makes things count,
steadies a fact into importance. Otherwise,

there it is among the moon rising,
a piece of paper being torn, starfish
at the bottom of the sea.
    Interesting how long it's taken me
to discover fulfillment
can be more trouble than it's worth.
Interesting, that as desire recedes
the world becomes pale yet clear.
I love knowing that even in rapture
part of the mind watches, amused.
    I love that there's a secret
behind every secret I've ever told.
I love twelve-year-old Scotch.
Before confessions of any sort,
a martini with a twist.
I love the wines
in my friend John's cellar,
the act of going down
and bringing them up,
and his vocabulary of taste
and aftertaste—tannin,
bouquet, tart—
I love how true experts speak
precisely, embody all the words.
And a beer for the big guy
at the end of the bar. He's my friend
too, on my father's side.
I love him for some old hurt
he's here to relieve.
    Who isn't selfish enough
to love zoos? Flamingos, baboons,
iguanas, newts.
Surely evolution has a sense of humor.
Surely the world would be something to love
if it weren't for us, insatiate,

our history of harm.
How hard even to love oneself,
all those things I've done
or dreamed of. Those vengeances.
     I love Don who is poor,
but I don't love the poor. I love *Jules
and Jim* more than I love *Casablanca,*
but only when I'm asked.
Isn't fairness for the timid?
I love the exacting prejudices
of the passionately thoughtful,
mercy earning its name,
transcending pity, which keeps
everyone small.
       I love my daughters out of
habit and conviction, my wife
for the long, undulating wave
of our friendship,
a few other women, a few men.
I love the number of people you can love
at the same time, one deep erotic love
radiating even to strangers, crippling
cynics, making a temporary sense
of the senseless, choreful day.
    When students fall in love with me
I want to tell them
I'm the dream that won't last;
there are more pleasures in the text.
So much eros in a normal room!
I love to use it
to make complexity joyous,
to heighten simple points.
    In spite of their lack of humor
I love Thoreau and Jesus, Marx,
Malcolm X. I love their obstinate courage,

Hunger Artists all, going forward
because the food they ate
tasted wrong, and the world was sad.
But I love the other heroes more,
Shakespeare and Picasso, Dickinson,
Beckett, Frost, wise dark players
among entropy and the ruins.
        I love the just-mowed grass
in spring, that good revision,
the clean odor of accomplishment.
I love the whale I saw
in the Caribbean, enormously itself.
And the fox who works the woods
behind my house, the envy of all of us:
deception without guilt.
I love the summer I decided to drive west
in a bad car.
I love the ferocity of certain dreams,
boulevards I've walked at midnight,
vulgarities made holy
in the mutual church of our bed.
    Those who've gotten away from me:
read this, and call.
Those whom I've hurt:
I wanted everything, or not enough;
it was all my fault.
    I love how the fireweed
came up on Mount St. Helens
through the crust of ash—
I think of this when my knees hurt,
when I feel like making an excuse.
I love that tyrants give birth
to the knives that slit their throats.
And I love the vigilant
who try to keep the tyrants dead,

knowing they rise with different names.
          (I'm saying all this to you,
my fiction, my one thing
that can be whole. I love what I might say,
the not yet felt or known.
In you there's room
for spires and orange rinds,
the mumbled, the suppresséd.
In you I could get lost.)
    I love the manners of jazz musicians,
the playing off of and the taking turns,
and the formality of chamber players,
I love that too, the tuxes and deep bows,
and the little aristocracy of the first
violinist and the conductor, the audience
complicitous, desiring such a world.
I love how pop songs seem profound
when we're in love,
though they wound us too sweetly,
never seriously enough.
I love the good home
clichés can find in an authentic voice.
          I love the secret life
of hornets, famous for their sting,
all day at home making paper,
building a place they must leave.
I love the night-blooming cereus
for its name alone,
and the amaryllis
that must be kept in the dark,
and once a year
blooms brilliantly large.
Just be natural, the innocent say.
Such latitude!

Permission to be wild, bizarre.
   I love intimacy, and accept
that concealment springs from it,
some partition of the heart
closing as it opens up.
After I asked my wife to marry me,
I hid behind a bush the next day
so she wouldn't see me,
and was thankful to Poe
and his Imp of the Perverse,
thankful, as it were, for a colleague.
Later, I loved telling her this,
laughter the sweetest agreement,
more conclusive than any yes.
   To give succor to the dying
and to kiss the diseased. To put a coin
in a leper's hand, and to hold that hand.
I love such love, and am its failure.
I love the selfless, but they're no fun,
like faraway planets,
shining, always shining.
I prefer a vanity that can be appealed to.
I love room enough not to be good.
   But what a pleasure it is
to feel righteous.
So rarely do I raise my voice,
what a pleasure to rant.
How seriously I'm taken then! Words
as bullets, emblems of the heart . . .
language every woman understands.
   I love to replace God
with all things tactile, responsive,
and I love artifice,
which is a way of being godly

if the product is good.
And science, its cures and its bomb;
I love with a fearful love
how far the mind has gone.
        Of all insects,
the thousand-legger.
Of flowers, the rose,
I cannot help it, the rose.
I love house more than country,
country more than space.
I love the thing chosen
and I love the illusion of choice.
        After the eyes offer up
their shynesses and deceits,
I look to mouths for the truth.
I love to see how temperament collects
in a smile, and often, before it happens,
it's possible to see cruelty,
a thin wire bent almost to a grin.
I love how lipstick can suggest
a grammar, and how, in sleep,
the mouth gives up its posture
like something defeated.
Isn't a morning kiss, then,
a kind of restoration, a love test
for the one who wakes first?
I love what we must forgive.
    So good to find them, the people
who've discovered fraudulence
in their lives, who've cast off, say,
a twenty-year lie.
I love how they listen to poems
as if words were necessary
daggers or balm, their faces proof
that the soul feeds on wild riffs,

every sort of truth-scrap, the blues.
I love that the normal condition
of the soul is to be starved.
       Of all seasons,
early autumn, the trees holding on
to what's theirs, and how nice
nobody's flunked yet, the classroom alive
with the beautiful ignorance of beginnings.
I love that the shy ones
sometimes grow wings,
and that the peacocks disappoint
when they begin to speak.
      I love to disappear on committees,
sneak out when the fastidious
begin to clean. I love to drift off
to where you are, love, when the solemn ones
need to make something clear.
Once in Chicago at the Hilton I slipped
an "I quit" note under my boss' door,
took a night flight home.
Whatever I love about my life
started there.
      When it comes to mixed feelings,
I love when the undertow begins,
as it must, to work against the flow.
Last week, accused of duplicity,
I knew I was guilty
of loving too few; there are truths
that can't be said out loud.
It's the singleminded who get
the most done, who rush right in.
I love a little hesitancy
before the plunge.
Liars, the whole lot of us.
      I love looking

for that slow car around 10 A.M.,
the mail-woman, Dorothy, who knows
I live for acceptances
and declarations of love.
Sometimes I'm out there waiting—
Thursday—the best day,
as any connoisseur knows.
I love how she leans out of her Nova
with the steering wheel on the right.
I love that she apologizes for junk,
that she knows the feel and look
of the personal, and how mock-sad she gets
when she has little to give.
Sundays I think of envelopes
being licked and stamped, mail in
transit, dream-mail,
change-one's-life mail. Sunday,
worst day of the week. And those
church bells ringing *stasis, stasis*.
                In the spacey boredom
of late afternoon, I love
that the casinos are open and near,
and sometimes after midnight, too,
for indulgence or danger's sake,
I love to walk through those electric doors
into the quick comfort
of slot sounds and sleaze.
I love to take my place among the prodigal
escapees screaming for sevens,
and one big time when everything went
my way, I loved placing all that cash
on my wife's sleeping body,
loved, come morning, to see her waken
like that, covered with luck.

I love the hour
before dinner, cheese on the cutting board,
white wine for her, something hard
for me. I love the rituals that bring us
together when sullenness persists,
how the dishes must be done,
the children helped toward bed.
I love how familiar bodies drift
back to each other
wordlessly, when the lights go out.
Oh we will die soon enough.
Not enough can be said
for a redemptive caress.

How good it's been to slide back
the heart's hood awhile, how fortunate
there's a heart and a covering for it,
and that whatever is still warm
has a chance.
I'm withholding things of course,
secrets I'll replay, alone,
when my bones get soft.
Even you have no place for them,
my spacious one, you who have existed
to resist me as I've made you up.
Do I sense you getting tired now?
Listen, my truest love, I've tried
to clear a late-century place for us
in among the shards. Lie down,
tell me what else you need.
Here is where loveliness can live
with failure, and nothing's complete.
I love how we go on.

Index